WHAT WOMEN SHOULD KNOW ABOUT

FACING FEAR

CHRISTIN DITCHFIELD

WHAT WOMEN SHOULD KNOW ABOUT FACING FEAR

FINDING FREEDOM
FROM ANXIOUS THOUGHTS,
NAGGING WORRIES,
AND CRIPPLING FEARS

WHAT WOMEN SHOULD KNOW ABOUT FACING FEAR

Finding Freedom from Anxious Thoughts, Nagging Worries, and Crippling Fears

ISBN 978-0-89112-372-9 LCCN2013023712

Printed in the United States of America

Published in association with William K. Jensen Literary Agency, 119 Bampton Court, Eugene, Oregon 97404.

Ditchfield, Christin.
What women should know about facing fear : finding freedom from anxious thoughts, nagging worries, and crippling fears / Christin Ditchfield.
pages cm
Includes bibliographical references.
ISBN 978-0-89112-372-9
1. Christian women--Religious life. 2. Fear--Religious aspects--Christianity. I. Title.
BV4527.D576 2013
248.8'43--dc23

2013023712

Cover design by Thinkpen Design, LLC Interior text design by Sandy Armstrong

Leafwood Publishers is an imprint of Abilene Christian University Press
1626 Campus Court, Abilene, Texas 79601
1-877-816-4455 www.leafwoodpublishers.com

13 14 15 16 17 18 / 7 6 5 4 3 2 1

Contents

To the Shepherd who called me
Out of the Valley of Humiliation
Into the Kingdom of Love—

You spoke tenderly to me,
You drew me with loving-kindness,
You delivered me from all my fears—
And captivated me with Your love.

My heart is Yours forever,
Always and completely.

Acknowledgments

I'm so deeply grateful to my precious family and friends for all their love and encouragement and prayers. You are such an important part of every book I write, every word I speak. I could not do what I do—I would not be who I am—without you.

A special thank you to my literary agent, Bill Jensen, and his wife, Sheila, for believing in me and the ministry God has called me to. Thank you to Gary Myers and the team at Leafwood for seeing the need for this book, sharing the vision—and turning it into a reality!

In writing a book for and about women, I can't help but be particularly mindful of the many women God has used to powerfully impact my heart and life. Especially those He brought alongside me, as I was first learning to find the courage to face my fears. There are those who came into my life for a moment—a brief, but very significant moment—"for such a time as this." There are some who were sent for a season. And there are some who are now and always will be my "forever" friends. There are those I've known personally and intimately and those I've never met—some who may even have lived and died before I was ever born, and yet whose testimonies and wise words have challenged me, encouraged me, and inspired me.

I wish I could list them all here (and part of me desperately wants to try), but I know in my heart that it just isn't possible. There are too many! And I'm sure I would accidentally leave some out. I can only thank God whenever I think of these amazing women, pray that He will bless them abundantly beyond all they can ask or imagine, and try to be a living tribute—a true reflection of all they have taught me, and the One they pointed me to.

Introduction

You gain strength, courage, and confidence by every experience in which you stop to look fear in the face. . . . You must do the thing you think you cannot do.

—Eleanor Roosevelt

Fear is something every one of us must face. It affects us all, in different ways, at different times, in different seasons of our lives. It comes in many shapes and sizes. And disguises. Sometimes it's that little gnawing creature, nibbling at the corners of our minds, making off with our peace a few crumbling pieces at a time. At others, it's a monster squatting on our chest, collapsing our lungs, making it impossible to breathe. Blocking our vision so we cannot see.

Some of our fears are admittedly a little silly, maybe even ridiculous, totally unreal. Others are terribly real. Some fears are life threatening—they can literally cost us our lives. Or keep us from taking action that would save our lives. Other fears keep us from living our lives. They rob us of the ability to truly experience life and enjoy life. Some fears keep us from becoming the women we long to be—the women we were meant to be. They keep us from doing what we really want to do, what we really need to do. Like writing a book. A book on facing fear, for instance.

For more than twenty years, I've been speaking at women's conferences and retreats, and many times the theme has been fear—facing our fear, finding God in the midst of our fear, choosing faith instead of fear. It's such a huge part of my own story, my own spiritual journey. I was thrilled when a publisher finally asked me to write about it! And then with a deadline looming, I suddenly realized:

I'm afraid to write this book. (Yes, I'm aware of the irony.)

It's just that this is such a vitally important subject. I'm afraid I might not do it justice. I'm afraid I might focus too much on one aspect of fear and not enough on another. I might accidentally leave something really important out. I'm afraid (okay, I *know*) that it's not possible to address from every angle every aspect of fear that every woman faces in one book—and I don't want any woman who reads this one to walk away without finding the help she needs.

I know I need to share more of my own story in this book than I have in any I've ever written—and that scares me, too. I want you to know that I know what it feels like, facing fear—I've really lived all of this. I'm not just preaching a bunch of pious platitudes. But it's hard to know what to share and how much. I'm afraid I might not get it right. I want to be real and relatable. What if I just sound paranoid and pathetic?

I've had the privilege of writing a number of books. It's always an incredible blessing whenever I hear that God has used something I've written to touch someone's heart or life. At the same time, there will always be people who don't like what I've written, people who twist things and take them out of context, people who misjudge or misunderstand me. Ultimately, I know that I write for an audience of One, that it's my heart's desire to do everything I do in His strength, for His glory, by His grace. Amen. He sees my heart. He knows the truth. That's what matters. But honestly, there are days when I'm afraid of the ugly words I might find in my in-box or in an online review. Days when I allow myself to get tied up in knots trying to anticipate every possible criticism—and avoid it by writing every sentence so perfectly that no one could possibly find fault. Hah!

Then there's the spiritual warfare that writing a book like this engenders. Fear is one of Satan's greatest weapons—one that seems to be especially effective against women. By standing up and speaking out, aren't I making myself a target? I've seen what he can do. Do I really want to risk provoking him? Haven't I been through enough already?

See what I mean? All this fear could be paralyzing. Truthfully, for a while, it was. But as the deadline drew closer, I had to do something. A lot of somethings, actually.

I had to face my fears—each one of them—and overcome them.

I had to put into practice everything God's been teaching me through the years, through His Word, and through the wise counsel and godly example of my brothers and sisters in Christ. The same things I want to share with you, the things we're going to talk about in this book.

Some of them I'm sure you know already—maybe (like me) you just need reminding. Others may be new. Still others may not be for you at all—but for you to share with a friend or family member, someone you know. Someone facing her own battle with fear.

Like you, like me.

See, that's the thing. The reality is that, when it comes to facing fear, no matter what our feelings tell us, no matter what our circumstances tell us, no matter what the enemy tells us, we are not alone. We are never alone. We have our sisters. And we have a strong and mighty Savior, who makes us this precious promise:

> Never will I leave you;
> never will I forsake you. (Heb. 13:5)

Or as the Amplified Bible puts it:

> He [God] Himself has said, I will not in any way fail you *nor* give you up *nor* leave you without support. [I will] not, [I will] not, [I will] not in any degree leave you helpless *nor* forsake *nor* let [you] down (relax My hold on you)! [Assuredly not!]

So on those days when your fears seem too much for you—when you just can't face them—slip your hand in His. Hide behind Him, if you want to. Better yet, climb up into His arms and rest your head on His chest. Listen to His heartbeat. Let His perfect love cast out all fear. And fill you with His perfect peace.

Let me show you how.

chapter one

Much Afraid and Me

One need not be a Chamber—to be Haunted—
One need not be a House—
The Brain has Corridors—surpassing
Material Place—

—Emily Dickinson

I have learned to tell people that I had a wonderful childhood. And it's true, as Obi-Wan would say, "from a certain point of view." I grew up in a wonderful family, surrounded by loving parents, doting grandparents, aunts and uncles, and cousins and siblings who were my playmates and best friends. We were all very close. We even lived in the same big house, and later in separate houses on the same property. We were a lot like the Waltons or the Ingalls on *Little House on the Prairie*—two of the top TV shows at the time. And like the Waltons and the Ingalls, we were a family of faith.

According to my baby book, my first word was "Jesus." Think how many times I would have had to have heard His name the first few months of my life for that to be so. I really can't remember a time when I didn't know Him. My grandmother used to tell me that she watched me preaching to my dollies when I was three.

Sounds like an idyllic childhood, doesn't it? Especially to my sweet friends who have suffered the horrors of abuse or abandonment and neglect. As an adult, I've learned to be very thankful for my family. I've learned to consider myself inordinately blessed. I've learned to focus on the happy memories of my childhood and (consciously or unconsciously) forget the rest.

It all seems so long ago and far away, and somehow disconnected from who I am today. Time and distance and life experience—these things give us perspective. But if you had asked me about my childhood when I was in my late teens or early twenties, I would have told you what I remembered most was fear.

As a child, I was filled with fear. All kinds of fear. I was afraid of the dark. I was afraid of crickets and frogs and spiders—which I seemed to encounter on an almost daily basis. I was absolutely terrified of dogs.

I knew there were no such things as monsters, but sometimes I could feel the presence of evil. I knew that the devil and demons were real.

Like all children, no matter how protective their parents, I saw things I shouldn't have in movies and on TV. My teachers, trying to encourage my love for reading, sometimes gave me books that were too grown up for me.

Many of my fears I kept to myself, hidden inside, where they silently tormented me. Others could not be hidden. When a creepy-crawly got in the house, for instance, or when we visited friends who had pets . . . or all the times I couldn't sleep at night.

My parents tried everything they could think of to help me. They talked to me, they listened to me, they prayed with me. Sometimes they came to my rescue. Other times they tried being firm, forcing me to face that day's fear in the hopes it would help me overcome it. Sometimes they tried reasoning with me. Sometimes they just held me.

Even as a child I knew that my fears were unreasonable and irrational. But that didn't make me less afraid. It made me feel ashamed. Even then I knew that God loved me, that He was watching over me and protecting me. I knew I was supposed to trust Him and not be afraid. But still I was afraid. And that made me ashamed. I knew that I should trust and obey my parents, and I wanted to—I really did. But often my fear got the better of me. And when it did, I was ashamed of the way I behaved.

I wanted desperately to be free from the fear that tormented me. But it wouldn't let go of me. And in some strange way I wouldn't let go of it.

As I got older, it just got worse. The more I learned about the world we live in, the more I realized it's a scary place. I began to understand that my parents weren't all-seeing, all-knowing, or all-powerful. They couldn't protect me from everything. Only God could. But would He? I started to wonder.

Talk about bad timing.

I will not fear, for you are ever with me and you will never leave me to face my perils alone.

—Thomas Merton

I was ten when my baby sister died. She was only three months old. It was sudden infant death syndrome, so we had no warning. As far as I knew, she was alive when I left for school that morning. But two hours later the school principal walked into my fifth-grade classroom, looking stricken. I knew something was wrong—very wrong—when she said my father had come to take me home.

In the days that followed, as excruciating as it must have been for them, my parents modeled for me extraordinary faith. I can still see my father sitting in the living room, listening to Handel's *Messiah* before we left for the funeral, tears streaming down his face, hands lifted in declaration: "I know that my Redeemer liveth. . . ." I can still see my mother at the graveside, tears streaming down her face, her hair blowing in the wind, as she stood in front of our friends and family and spoke of God's faithfulness, of her love for and trust in Him.

But, for the first time, I was seeing true suffering—anguish and grief and pain—up close, and I could never look at life the same way again. I could never look at God the same way again. When you know that sometimes He lets babies die, how can you feel safe? How can you be sure what He might let happen to you or your family next?

By the time I was in junior high, the focus of my fear had shifted dramatically. It had taken a huge turn inward. I had never really been comfortable with kids my own age; I was "different," I didn't really fit in. I was awkward and unattractive. I felt extremely self-conscious. I became horrifically shy. I hated being put in new environments and unfamiliar circumstances—not knowing where to go, what to say, or what to do. I was so afraid of making mistakes, getting things wrong, of falling or failing in any way. I was afraid of the embarrassment, the humiliation, the ridicule, the rejection. It didn't help that by this time we'd moved away from the loving enclave of extended family through a number of different cities and states, churches, schools.

I felt like my life was one long nightmare. Every day brought the prospect of some new torture I was desperate to avoid, leading to yet another conflict with my loving and supportive, but increasingly frustrated, parents.

Like the time we visited a new library. At first it was heaven! I loved books more than anything . . . reading was my escape. When we walked in, I'd taken note of the sign near the front door that said patrons could check out up to thirty books at a time. I then spent an hour in the young adult section, picking out fifty or sixty novels that looked intriguing to me. It took me another forty-five minutes painstakingly sorting through the stack, narrowing it down to what I hoped were the best of the best—the top thirty. I was deliberating between the last two contenders when my mom appeared and announced that it was time to go. She seemed a little harried, trying to corral my other siblings, and she wanted me to go ahead and check out by myself. Only this was our first visit and I didn't have a library card. I would have to ask for one. Meaning I'd have to actually talk to the librarian. Out loud. At that moment I honestly thought I would rather die.

I couldn't believe my mom would ask me to do such a thing. She knew how I felt. Trying not to make a scene, I just shook my head and mouthed the word "no." Firmly. And repeatedly. With more than a hint of exasperation in her voice, my mother, grabbing hold of my five-year-old sister by the arm, said, "Christin, it's simple. You walk up to the counter and say, 'May I have a library card, please.'"

I shook my head again, frantically this time. "No . . . . I can't . . . no. You do it. Please, please, please!" At this point, I was begging.

When she refused, I lost it. "Fine!" I said, "I'll put them all back!" And I meant it. I would rather put every single book back on the shelf than have to speak to the librarian. For whatever reason, my mom caved-in that day. She went and got me my library card.

But another day it was a different story.

When I was in ninth grade we started attending a new church, and my parents thought it would be good for me to get involved with the high school youth group. At the very least, they wanted me to attend Sunday school. Of course I didn't want to go, but my parents insisted. Of all things, this youth group was so large that it had to meet at another facility, several blocks away from the main church building. That just made it so much worse. I would be completely alone on that campus, all by myself, without anyone I knew. That first Sunday we argued all the way there. Then to my horror, my parents pulled up to the front of the building, ordered me out of the car, and drove away. I stood on the sidewalk sobbing. Shaking so hard I couldn't breathe. I could not have been more terrified of walking into a room full of people I didn't know, trying to make conversation with them.

It takes courage to grow up and
become who you really are.

—e. e. cummings

Of course I couldn't stand there all day. Any minute someone else would arrive and see me crying. All I could do was wipe away the tears, take a deep breath, and walk inside. But that year, in part because of some of the experiences I had in that youth group, things began to change.

Being a teenager, I started questioning everything I'd ever believed, challenging everything I'd ever been taught. Was my faith really my own—or was I just carrying on a beloved family tradition?

Did I really believe in Jesus for myself? Did I know Him? Did I love Him? Did I trust Him? And if I did, shouldn't I want to know Him more? Love Him more? Trust Him more?

I decided I did. I should. I would.

That's when I started really pursuing a relationship with Jesus, seeking after God for myself. I saved up my babysitting money to buy a student Bible in place of the children's Bible I'd had since I was five. I got up an hour earlier every day so that I could make myself a cup of coffee and read my Bible and pray. I worked on memorizing verses that were meaningful to me.

I especially loved the Psalms. So many of them, I discovered, were about finding courage in times of fear. I listened to praise and worship music as I got ready to face the day.

And then throughout the day, like the psalmist, I cried out to God whenever I was afraid.

I wasn't sure at first what would happen. I didn't know what—if anything—to expect. But to my wonder and amazement, I found that when I called, He answered me. He comforted me. He strengthened me. Time after time, I learned that I could trust Him. That even if He allowed difficult or painful things to happen, He would be with me—and that going through those trials with Him was far better than facing them on my own. I also came to the realization that I didn't just have fears—I had a spirit of fear. I needed to be set free. I began asking God to deliver me and He did. The difference was night and day.

> Perfect love casts out fear. (1 John 4:18 ESV)

Ultimately, that's what happened to me. I fell in love with Jesus. He had been living in my heart all this time. But, as a child, I couldn't even begin to understand what this relationship would mean to me as an adult. Now I knew—or I was beginning to. Some people would say this was when I rededicated my life to Christ and made an adult commitment of my life to Him.

The way you overcome shyness is to become so wrapped up in something that you forget to be afraid.

—Lady Bird Johnson

About this time, my grandmother gave me two books that had been a great help to her when she first gave her heart to Jesus: a daily devotional called *Streams in the Desert*, and *Hinds Feet on High Places* by Hannah Hurnard. I devoured both.

If you've read *Hinds Feet on High Places*, you'll remember it tells the story of a young woman called Much Afraid who lives in the Valley of Humiliation, where she is constantly tormented by Fear. Much Afraid longs to escape to the Kingdom of Love—but it lies far away, high up in the lofty mountains. And Much Afraid is crippled. One day the Chief Shepherd, who lives in the Kingdom of Love Himself—and is in fact the Son of the King—invites Much Afraid on a journey that will lead her there. He promises to make her feet like hinds' (deer) feet, so that she can leap across the mountain heights and says He will send her two companions to help her along the way. Much Afraid is taken aback when she learns her companions' names: Sorrow and Suffering. But she soon discovers just how helpful they can be, how necessary to achieving her dream of reaching the Kingdom of Love and receiving her hinds' feet and her new name.

I instantly connected with the character of Much Afraid, as my grandmother knew I would. I related to her struggles, her trials and temptations. I had no idea then how much my journey would mirror hers. How much I would come to know her companions, Sorrow and Suffering, or that one day, like Much Afraid, I would learn to call them dear friends.

Little by little, day by day, God was doing a new work in my heart and life—transforming me from the inside out. The more I knew Him, the more I loved Him. The more I loved Him, the more I wanted to share His love with those around me. But to do that, I'd have to be willing to open my mouth and speak to them.

People who know me now have a hard time believing that I was ever Much Afraid. I am, after all, as my official biography reads, "an accomplished educator, author and conference speaker, and internationally syndicated radio host." I travel all over the country speaking to thousands of women each year. Every day of my life I do dozens of things that used to be unthinkable to me. Things that would have terrified me. Things I could never have imagined myself bold enough or brave enough to do.

And it's all because of Him.

> I sought the LORD, and he answered me;
> he delivered me from all my fears. (Ps. 34:4)

It's been an amazing journey, full of ups and downs, twists and turns, stops and starts—challenges and adventures all along the way. There have been times when I've been under fierce attack, when the enemy of my soul has seen an area of vulnerability and come at me hard. In my adult life, there have been seasons when I've had to do battle with fear again. I've experienced panic attacks and night terrors and the like. But those times have been few and far between.

I can honestly say that fear is no longer a dominant theme, a major issue, in my life today. I have to face it from time to time, like everybody else. But I've had more chance to practice than most people. I guess that's a good thing. And I've learned quite a few things along the way. I'm still learning every day.

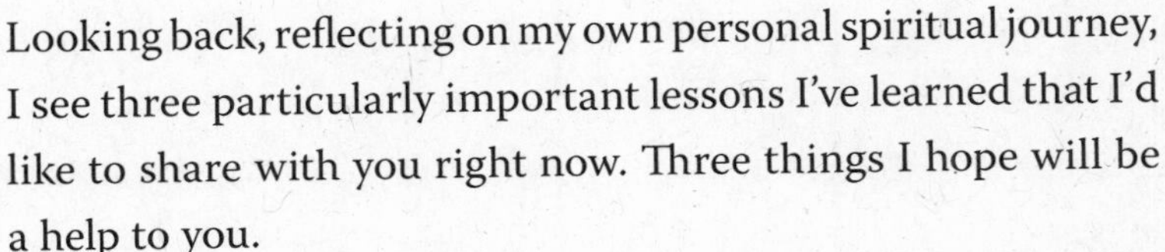

Take chances, make mistakes. That's how you grow. Pain nourishes your courage. You have to fail in order to practice being brave.

—Mary Tyler Moore

Looking back, reflecting on my own personal spiritual journey, I see three particularly important lessons I've learned that I'd like to share with you right now. Three things I hope will be a help to you.

1. God used my fear to draw me to Him. Some of the sweetest, deepest, richest experiences I've ever had in my relationship with Him, the times when I have felt His presence most powerfully, when I have heard His voice most clearly, came about as a direct result of the suffering I endured. The desperation I felt. The determination to press in and grab hold of Him—only to find that it was He who'd grabbed hold of me.

2. It is possible to be set free from fear. Free from its stranglehold. Free from its domination and control. I've experienced it myself. I've been set free. Yes, sometimes I still *feel* fear, sometimes I still *battle* fear, sometimes I'm still *tempted* to fear, but I don't *live* in fear. Not anymore. It's hard to put into words the difference that makes.

3. When I feel afraid now, I see it as an alert, an indicator, or a warning. It helps me know that something isn't right. Either I am in some kind of danger and I need to be on guard, or I have some heart issues that I need to deal with. Once again it brings me to the feet of Jesus.

Let me share one example:

Just last year I found myself in a really dark place emotionally and spiritually. It felt like I had been there for a really long time. I realized I was afraid I might never get out of it. More than afraid. I was terrified. What if I was stuck here forever? What if I never got free? How could I go on living like this?

This was a whole different kind of fear.

"*But* God, . . ." as one of my dear friends likes to say.

But God, in His great love and tender mercy, whispered some of the same sweet words He first spoke to my heart so many years ago. He led me to Habakkuk 3:19, the verse that inspired *Hinds Feet on High Places,* which in the Amplified Bible reads:

> The Lord God is my Strength, my personal bravery, *and* my invincible army; He makes my feet like hinds' feet and will make me to walk [not to stand still in terror, but to walk] *and* make [spiritual]

> progress upon my high places [of trouble, suffering, or responsibility]!

It's my prayer that He will strengthen and encourage your heart—as He has mine—as we take the next steps of our journey together.

Bible Study

At the end of each chapter you'll find questions like these to help you reflect on the biblical principles we've discussed and apply them to your own life. You may want to record your responses in a separate notebook or journal.

1. How would you describe your own childhood? Were you fearful? What kinds of things were you afraid of?

2. How much would you say fear is a factor in your life right now? How often is it something you battle?

   ☐ Once in a while
   ☐ Fairly frequently
   ☐ Constantly
   ☐ It's crippling me

   Does it seem to be getting better or worse over time?

3. Can you think of a time when your fears proved to be unfounded, when you dreaded or worried or agonized over something that never happened—or that turned out to be a nonissue?

4. Can you think of a time when your fears were realized? Was it as bad as you thought it would be? Better? Worse?

5. Read Psalm 34 in its entirety. You might want to underline key words and phrases in your Bible or make note of them in your journal.

   a. In Psalm 34:1–3, what is the psalmist determined to do?

b. What does the psalmist testify to—what has he witnessed, what has he experienced, what does he know to be true—according to verses 4–7, 15, 17–19?

c. Can you remember a time in the past when God helped you face your fears or overcome them?

d. What part of the psalmist's testimony speaks most to your heart today? How does it encourage you?

6. Choose one of the following verses to memorize and meditate on this week:

Psalm 23 Psalm 34:4

Psalm 46:1
Psalm 28:7
Psalm 40:1–3
Psalm 71:14–18

7. Take a few moments to record any further thoughts or reflections in your journal.

chapter two

Faces of Fear

To fear is one thing. To let fear grab you by the tail and swing you around is another.

—Katherine Paterson

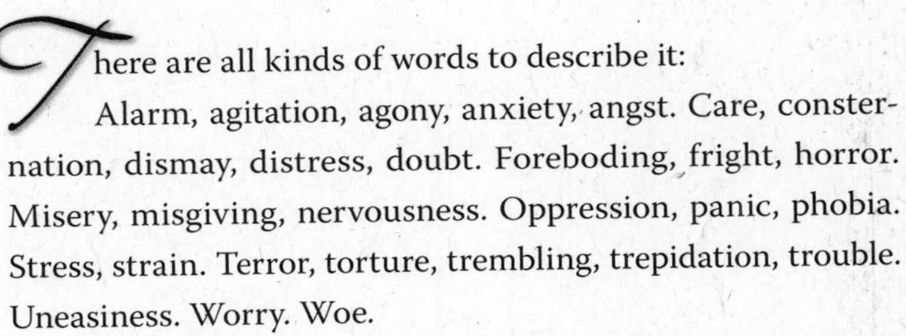

There are all kinds of words to describe it:

Alarm, agitation, agony, anxiety, angst. Care, consternation, dismay, distress, doubt. Foreboding, fright, horror. Misery, misgiving, nervousness. Oppression, panic, phobia. Stress, strain. Terror, torture, trembling, trepidation, trouble. Uneasiness. Worry. Woe.

Fear has many different names, different faces. It comes in different shapes and sizes—and disguises. It likes to pretend to be one thing, when deep down it's really another.

Some fears seem perfectly understandable, socially acceptable, even fashionable. (In another era we might say "feminine"—or rather, men might.) Others fill us with shame—and the added fear that our secret fear will somehow be uncovered.

There are fears that seem to be relatively minor, little hindrances or hiccups that happen to come up from time to time. Others are huge obstacles—obsessive, even compulsive, all-consuming fears that dominate us and threaten to destroy all we hold dear.

Most of our fears and worries fall somewhere in between. Some fears come and go. Some settle in for a season. Some seem to last for a lifetime.

There's really no objective scale for measuring fear—determining how great it is, how serious or significant it is, how real or rational it is (or isn't). Or even how relevant.

Like beauty, it's in the eye of the beholder. Or maybe it's the power it holds over the prisoner.

Take the fear of flying, for instance. Millions of people are afraid of flying (or, more accurately, afraid of dying in a plane crash). It makes the top ten in just about any "greatest fears" list.

But millions of other people think nothing of it. These are the people who are quick to volunteer that you're more likely to die in a car accident a half mile from your house than in a plane crash. Even though no one has asked for this information—ever. As if it could or should make you feel less afraid, when all it really does is make you feel embarrassed or ashamed—and more than a little defensive. If only you could pull out some snappy statistics to point out the irrationality of *their* fears (whatever their fears are)—because you know they have them. We all do.

But if you never need to get on a plane, how significant is your fear of flying, really?

Okay, but what if your job requires you to fly on a regular basis? How significant is it then?

What if your health or the health of a loved one required you to fly somewhere for treatment?

What if you've always wanted to go on a mission trip or a service project overseas?

What if you have dreams of traveling the world, experiencing different cultures and cuisines?

What if your children or grandchildren live far away?

What if God has put it on your heart to go somewhere or do something—anything—and you won't do it, you refuse. Because you won't get on a plane. How significant is your fear of flying then?

We could ask these questions of any fear, really . . . the point I'm trying to make is that it's all relative. What may be a big issue for one person may not be for another. What might be a minor inconvenience for one person might lead to sin and disobedience for another. None of us can or should (though let's face it, sometimes we do) presume to know what another woman's greatest fears are—or how she should be facing them. It's really personal. And I don't just mean private. I mean individual. Unique to her and her spiritual journey, her relationship with Jesus.

Someone might see evidence of fear in our lives and be quick to say, "You need to deal with that right away! You need to [do this or that or the other . . .]" But God might see that the fear is a symptom of something else. He might see an even greater fear, one with deeper roots, one with more significant impact that He wants us to address first—because He knows that when we take this one down, the rest will follow.

Those of us who want to be free from fear have to come to Him on our own. We have to lay our hearts open before Him and ask Him to reveal to us what He sees. Yes, there may be godly counselors He uses, close friends or family members who can help us. But each of us is responsible to seek Him for ourselves, to carefully weigh all of the input and advice we receive in the light of His truth. Only He knows which fears He wants us to face when and what steps He wants us to take—how fast or how slow. What battles He wants us to fight and which weapons we should use.

For this reason, I'm resisting the urge to turn this book into an encyclopedia of fears, a handbook of surefire remedies and helpful hints in alphabetical order. Because that may not be helpful to you.

Instead, in this chapter, we will take a look at some common fears—kinds of fears—that most women face. And in later chapters we'll get into some specific strategies for facing and overcoming fear. But I'm going to try my hardest to stick to principles that any woman can apply in her own way to any situation, to any worry or fear she may face.

And I'm going to encourage you again and again to take all of these things to Jesus. Talk to Him about them. Listen to Him. And "do whatever He tells you" (John 2:5).

If you can keep your head when
all about you are losing theirs, it's just
possible you haven't grasped the situation.

—Jean Kerr

Without a doubt, there are some fears that, as women, we all seem to share. And most of them are interrelated. Like the fear of failure and the fear of success. Many of us are afraid to fail—afraid to mess up, to miss the mark, to make a mistake. Some of us are afraid that if we do somehow succeed, we'll only be setting the bar higher. We'll have to face new challenges, new obstacles. What if we can't overcome them? What if we fail? It may also have occurred to us that success brings a bigger spotlight—and a bigger glare.

For many women the fear of humiliation is even greater than the fear of failure or success. The Bible calls this the "fear of man." It's that desperate need for others' approval, affirmation, appreciation, or admiration. It's the desire to avoid criticism, ridicule, or rejection, to avoid social embarrassment or public humiliation—at all costs. No one wants to be mocked, misjudged, or misunderstood, disliked or discussed (okay, gossiped about) behind their backs.

That's because deep down, many of us are deeply insecure. We have a terrible fear of inadequacy. This is a huge one for most women today. It's the fear of not being "__________ enough." Not tall enough or small enough or thin enough or curvy enough. Not beautiful or sexy enough. Not smart enough, not kind enough, not important enough. Not educated enough. Not artistic or creative enough. Not organized or coordinated or put-together enough. Not diligent enough. Not strong enough. Not patient enough. Not loving enough. Not spiritual enough. Not good enough. Whatever it is, whatever we are, it's not enough. There are all kinds of reasons we feel this way, including the fact that we have a multi-billion-dollar industry built on convincing us of it every single day—so that we'll buy this product or that service or have some procedure done. It's truly diabolical. But we're so afraid that if we're not enough and we can't find a way to be enough, we'll lose whatever it is we've still got.

And that brings us to the mother of all fears, the fear that spawns so many of its own subcategories or kinds of fears: the fear of loss. Such as . . .

Loss of security: We're worried about our finances, our jobs, our homes. We have fears for our safety and well-being and the safety and well-being of those we love.

Loss of control: We're afraid we might lose the ability to stay on top of all our responsibilities and keep everything together, running smoothly. We're afraid we might lose control of our emotions. Our sanity. We're afraid we might lose control over dozens of things that—in reality—we have no control over anyway.

Loss of a loved one: We fear losing a parent or sibling, a child, a spouse. And not just losing them to death. We fear losing a parent or grandparent to dementia, for instance, or a child to reckless behavior and rebellion, or a spouse to divorce. Many of us also fear we'll lose loved ones before they've responded to the Gospel, so we fear their spiritual death as well as their physical death.

Loss of relationship / loss of community: We're afraid of being abandoned, neglected, rejected, friendless, and alone. We don't want to lose others' acceptance, our sense of connection, the feeling of belonging, being valued, needed, or loved.

Loss of health and life itself: We fear aging, the ravages of time. We fear physical pain and suffering, disease and disability and death. We also fear the death of our hopes and dreams, the loss of all the things we know now that we'll never experience or accomplish.

And these are just a few! Really, it's a wonder we can get out of bed in the morning. If we didn't have to go to the bathroom, some of us wouldn't.

The hardest years in life are those
between ten and seventy.

—Helen Hayes, at age 82

Believe it or not, fear does have an upside. Because not all fear is bad. There is a healthy kind of fear and a proper time and place for it. That heart-pounding sensation is meant to alert us when we're in danger. It's supposed to warn us when we're about to engage in behavior that could put us in harm's way. The right kind of fear at the right time can keep us alive. But the wrong kind of fear—unhealthy, unbalanced fear—can keep us from living life the way God intended.

That's why more than four hundred times in the Bible God says to us, "Fear not!"—including all the variations on the theme:— "Do not be anxious." "Do not worry." "Do not be troubled." "Do not be afraid." "Be bold." "Have courage." "Take heart." "Stand firm."

In Romans 8:15, Paul reminds us that when we first trusted in Christ, we became part of God's family. God gave us His Spirit to live within us. This is not a spirit that makes us "a slave again to fear." We used to be slaves to sin, slaves to fear. But not anymore. We have become children of God, and the Spirit living in us cries out to Him in faith and trust: "Abba—Father!"

In 2 Timothy 1:7, Paul tells us again that God has not given us a "spirit of fear; but of power, and of love, and of a sound mind" (KJV).

There is one kind of fear—and only one—that God wants us to have. One kind of fear He wants us to live in. It's the best kind, the healthiest kind: what the Bible calls the fear of the Lord.

Remember all those words for fear I mentioned at the beginning of the chapter? I left out a few. If you look up "fear" in the dictionary, you'll also find:

Awe. Wonder. Reverence. Worship.

> What does the LORD your God ask of you but to fear the LORD your God, to walk in all his ways, to love him, to serve the LORD your God with all your heart and with all your soul. (Deut. 10:12)

Proverbs 9:10 explains,

> The fear of the LORD is the beginning of wisdom,
> and knowledge of the Holy One is understanding.

When we choose to fear God—when we reverence and respect Him, when we trust Him and obey Him, when we love Him and serve Him—we choose to live in His will and under His protection. We don't need to fear anything or anyone else.

> Those who live in the shelter of the Most High
> will find rest in the shadow of the Almighty.
> This I declare about the Lord:
> He alone is my refuge, my place of safety;
> he is my God, and I trust him.
> For he will rescue you from every trap
> and protect you from deadly disease.
> He will cover you with his feathers.
> He will shelter you with his wings.
> His faithful promises are your armor
> and protection.
> Do not be afraid of the terrors of the night,
> nor the arrow that flies in the day.
> Do not dread the disease that stalks in darkness,
> nor the disaster that strikes at midday.
> Though a thousand fall at your side,
> though ten thousand are dying around you,
> these evils will not touch you. . . .
> If you make the Lord your refuge,
> if you make the Most High your shelter,
> no evil will conquer you;
> no plague will come near your home.

> For he will order his angels
> to protect you wherever you go. . . .
> The LORD says, "I will rescue those who love me.
> I will protect those who trust in my name.
> When they call on me, I will answer;
> I will be with them in trouble.
> I will rescue and honor them.
> I will reward them with a long life
> and give them my salvation."
> (Ps. 91:1–7, 9–11, 14–16 NLT)

In the darkest of nights cling to the assurance that God loves you, that He always has advice for you, a path that you can tread and a solution to your problem—and you will experience that which you believe. God never disappoints anyone who places his trust in Him.

—Basilea Schlink

Proverbs 31:30 tells us,

> Charm is deceptive, and beauty is fleeting;
> but a woman who fears the LORD is to be praised.

The Bible gives us some powerful examples of what this looks like—what "a woman who fears the LORD" looks like—in real life. And what a difference it makes. I'm thinking of one woman in particular. A woman whose fear of God made her incredibly brave and full of faith.

If we had known her back then, I'm not sure that you and I would have seen in her what God saw. Okay, I'm pretty sure we *wouldn't* have. We probably would have tried not to see her at all. We would have crossed to the other side of the street, avoided eye contact, said nothing to her or about her—if we were being nice, that is.

Because Rahab was a prostitute.

We don't know how she came to be one. But we know that then as now, even in cultures where it's tolerated or accepted, the world's "oldest profession" is not highly regarded. Women who practice it aren't among society's honored, admired, and respected. They're outcasts—despised and rejected.

Rahab lived in Jericho, a wicked city God told His people to destroy. The Children of Israel were finally taking possession of the Promised Land. They'd sent spies to go on ahead and check things out. Two of them arrived in Jericho, slipping in among the riffraff on the seedier side of the city. They ended up staying at Rahab's house.

Somehow the king of Jericho heard about these men and sent soldiers to arrest them. But Rahab had already hidden them on the roof of her house, which was built along the wall of the city.

At first we're not sure why. Why would this woman risk her life for these men, these strangers? Why would she defy the king? Betray her own country, her own people?

This is what she told the spies, after she sent the soldiers on a wild goose chase:

> I know that the LORD has given this land to you and that a great fear of you has fallen on us, so that all who live in this country are melting in fear because of you. We have heard how the LORD dried up the water of the Red Sea for you when you came out of Egypt, and what you did to Sihon and Og, the two kings of the Amorites east of the Jordan, whom you completely destroyed. When we heard of it, our hearts melted and everyone's courage failed because of you, for the LORD your God is God in heaven above and on the earth below. (Josh. 2:9–11)

Her countrymen heard what God had done, and they were terrified. Rahab heard, and she was filled with awe and wonder. Reverence and worship. When the spies came to her door, she knew it was her chance to declare herself to be on the Lord's side—and to seek His favor and protection.

> Now then, please swear to me by the LORD that you will show kindness to my family, because I have shown kindness to you. Give me a sure sign that you will spare the lives of my father and mother, my brothers and sisters, and all who belong to them—and that you will save us from death. (Josh. 2:12–13)

Though she was the "enemy," a foreigner, a woman, a prostitute (and every one of those things could have been considered a huge strike against her)—she wasn't afraid to speak up. She wasn't afraid to ask, to make her request known. She had such faith in God's justice, in His goodness, in His mercy and grace. A faith His own people rarely displayed.

She feared God, and, because she feared God, she feared nothing else. Not her own king or countrymen, not the risk to her own life, not the possibility of rejection or ridicule from the Israelites, not the difficulties of surviving and starting over, trying to find a new life.

She had no fear. Just faith.

Of course the spies immediately agreed to Rahab's request. And, that night, she tied a scarlet cord at her window to lower them down outside the city wall. The men asked her to leave the cord hanging there, to mark the place where she and her family would take refuge. And she did. That scarlet cord was a symbol, a witness, a testimony to her fear of God—and her faith in God.

A week later, when the walls of Jericho fell, Rahab and all her family were saved. Rahab had no idea that her story had just begun. When it all started, she was just hoping not to die. But God had been setting a plan in motion not just to lead His people to victory over Jericho but to rescue Rahab—in every sense of the word. To redeem her and restore her.

In the same way that centuries later Jesus would go out of his way to encounter the Woman at the Well, God went out of His way to reach into the city of Jericho and draw Rahab out—because she feared Him. She belonged to Him. She was His.

She didn't know it yet, but it was true: Rahab belonged with God and His people. And they weren't going on without her. By hiding His spies and hanging that scarlet cord, Rahab may have thought she was making a deal with God, but God wanted to make an even better deal with her:

> "Come now, let us reason together," says the LORD. "Though your sins are like scarlet, they shall be as white as snow." (Isa. 1:18)

God gave her so much more than she bargained for. He gave her a new life. A new country, a new people, a new faith. A new love.

He gave her a husband and a son. And then He made her part of His Son's family tree. Rahab is one of only five women mentioned in the genealogy of Jesus (Matt. 1:5). She's included with all of the great men and women of the Bible in the Hebrews 11 "Hall of Faith" (v. 31). Of all the illustrations he could have used, James chose her story as an example of what it means to have a real, living, and active faith (James 2:24–26).

Rahab teaches us that we fight fear with fear. We conquer fear with fear. We overcome unhealthy fear, tormenting fear, paralyzing fear with healthy fear, righteous fear, holy fear. The fear of the Lord.

Rahab reminds us that it doesn't matter where we've come from or where we've been, what mistakes we've made or how we've sinned. It's not about our successes or failures, what we've won or lost. It's not about whether the world or the church or our own families admire us or despise us. It doesn't matter whether we're even close to "enough"—by anyone's standards, including our own.

What matters is our heart's condition. Do we fear God? Do we love Him? Do we trust Him?

If we do, then we know:

> Those who look to him are radiant;
> their faces are never covered in shame.
> (Ps. 34:5)

Bible Study

1. Look up Psalm 55:6. Spend a few moments in quiet reflection, asking God to shine the light of His truth as you examine your heart before Him. Make a list of your top five or top ten worries or anxieties right now. If you don't having pressing concerns that come to mind, then list your top five or top ten fears.

2. Let's try to go a little deeper. We talked about how "fear of flying" is really "fear of dying in a terrifying plane crash." Rewrite the items on your list, using words that more accurately describe what you're really afraid of—what you're afraid of will or won't happen. Be as real and as honest as you can. It might take you a few tries, but it's worth it. If you don't know what the fear is, you can't face it—or fight it.

3. Look up each of the following Scriptures and take notes on the wisdom or instruction or encouragement they offer.

a) 1 Peter 5:7
b) Psalm 130:5; Micah 7:7
c) Proverbs 3:5–6
d) James 1:5
e) Psalm 37:4
f) Psalm 37:5–6
g) Psalm 37:23–24
h) Psalm 37:25; Philippians 4:19
i) John 3:16; John 14:2–3; Revelation 21:3–4

How do these verses speak to the worries or fears you described above?

4. Choose one of the verses above, one of the following verses, or one mentioned previously in the chapter, to memorize and meditate on this week:

Psalm 130:3–4
Psalm 147:11
Psalm 91:1–2
Deuteronomy 31:8
Psalm 91:14–16
2 Thessalonians 3:16

5. Take a few moments to record any further thoughts or reflections in your journal.

chapter three

Failing and Flailing

How very little can be done under the spirit of fear.

—Florence Nightingale

A couple of years ago I was interviewed on a radio program. The friendly host was chatting with me about a book I had just written, *A Way with Words: What Women Should Know about the Power They Possess.* We got to talking about the differences between men and women and how we communicate, and then the host posed an unexpected question. He said,

> Christin, I think we'd probably agree that there's ONE temptation that all men seem vulnerable to, ONE sin that all men seem to struggle with—and that's sexual sin. But I don't get the feeling it's that way for women, that women as a whole have ONE particular weakness or sin, one major area that they ALL struggle with. What do you think?

Now this was not the subject of my book—or any book I'd ever written. It wasn't in the list of questions my publisher had provided to us both ahead of time, questions for which I'd carefully prepared what I hoped would be thoughtful, informative, helpful answers. Looking back, I don't think the host was trying to put me on the spot. I don't think he really expected me to have an answer. He was just making conversation. Thinking out loud—into a microphone. On live radio.

But as I opened my mouth to speak (I had to say something), a thought dropped into my head. God reminded me of an observation I'd made time and time again. And so I said:

> Actually, I do. I do think nearly all women are vulnerable to one particular temptation, one particular sin. I think our big issue is control. The temptation to resort to manipulation in an effort to gain control.

Don't get mad at me yet! I went on to explain that as women, one of our greatest needs is for security. We want to feel safe. We want to *be* safe. We want the people we love to be safe. And happy and healthy. We want the world to be a safe and happy place. But it isn't. And it hasn't been, since the Garden of Eden.

That's when things first went horribly wrong.

It sounded like an innocent question. The serpent asked Eve, "Did God really say, 'You must not eat from any tree in the garden?'" But the serpent was crafty—more crafty than any of the creatures God had made. He skillfully drew the first unsuspecting woman into a conversation that would lead to deadly results.

Eve obligingly explained God's command and the consequence of eating from the tree of the knowledge of good and evil. But the serpent contradicted her. "You will not surely die," he hissed. "For God knows that when you eat of it, your eyes will be opened, and you will be like God, knowing good and evil" (Gen. 3:4–5).

What is the serpent really saying here? That God is wrong, that He's untruthful, that He can't be trusted. He's saying that God would deliberately withhold something good from His children out of spite. In other words, "God knows this is really good and He doesn't want you to have it." The accusation is that God is unjust and unfair and unkind.

Eve listened to the serpent, and she believed him. She disobeyed God. And that sin ushered in all the evil, all the wickedness, all the vile and despicable things that fill us with fear and horror today.

Over the years, Satan's strategy hasn't changed much. He whispers the same things to our hearts today. He takes any and every opportunity to malign the character of God and undermine our faith in Him. In John 8:44, Jesus said the devil "was a murderer from the beginning, not holding to the truth, for there is no truth in him. When he lies, he speaks his native language, for he is a liar and the father of lies."

When we listen to those lies, we let fear rule our hearts instead of faith.

We're afraid things won't turn out the way we want them to, so we try to take charge. We try to take over. We take matters into our own hands—instead of trusting them to God.

We plot, we plan, we scheme. We whine, we pout, we cry. We lie. We nag, we fuss. We push, we prod, we promote, we campaign. We flatter, we flirt. We order, we insist, we demand.

We give the silent treatment. We withhold love and affection or approval. The list goes on and on. We're bound and determined to get our own way.

Honestly, sometimes our motivation is greed or selfishness or ambition—even if we tell ourselves that we're doing what we're doing for the good of others. But for many women, if not most, when you dig deep enough, what you find at the root of it all is some kind of fear. One of those fears we just talked about in the last chapter.

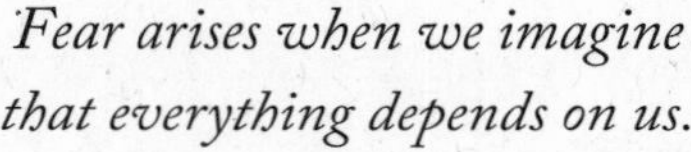

Fear arises when we imagine
that everything depends on us.

—Elisabeth Elliot

And manipulation is just one of the unsuccessful strategies we sometimes resort to in our failing and flailing attempts to battle fear. As we look at some of the others, you may notice that the issue of control is a recurring theme.

Perfectionism: Many of us turn to perfectionism for our salvation—in more ways than one. If we can just be perfect, then everyone will love us and appreciate us and approve of us. No one will criticize us, judge us, ridicule or reject us. We'll never be embarrassed, never make any mistakes, never fail, never hurt or disappoint anyone. Never let anyone down. Anyone, including ourselves. Including God. If we can just be perfect, we won't have to be afraid of all those ugly feelings we sense may be lurking deep inside—jealousy, envy, insecurity, bitterness, unforgivingness. If we can just be perfect, then we'll be enough. Enough to please others, enough to please ourselves. Enough to please God. To show our sincerity and devotion, to prove our worthiness. To earn our salvation. Some of us figure out pretty quickly that it's not possible—we can't be perfect, no matter how hard we try. But instead of embracing that reality, finding freedom in it, and reveling in God's mercy and grace, we just choose a different strategy—like the next one.

Risk avoidance: This one can be tough to spot sometimes, because it looks a lot like wisdom. It looks like we're being careful and cautious, thoughtful, considerate, deliberate. We have what we think are very reasonable, very logical, maybe even very spiritual-sounding arguments to support our decisions. Another person making the same decision could be doing so for all the right reasons. But our reason is fear. We are avoiding people, relationships, places, situations and circumstances, opportunities and experiences, because we are afraid. Afraid of conflict, afraid of failure, afraid of danger, afraid of pain, afraid of loss. So we do our best to avoid it—and make sure our loved ones do, too.

People pleasing: We just want everyone to be happy. More than that, we want them to like us—really like us. So we'll do whatever they want us to do, be whoever they want us to be. Our favorite word is "yes"—because we've learned that other people don't like to be told no. We fear their anger, their judgment, their criticism. We fear being alienated from the people who give us our sense of identity and community and family, our sense of belonging. Even if we don't like the friends we have, we prefer them to being friendless and alone. So we keep saying yes. But when we say yes to everyone else, we can't say yes to God. We can't say yes to who He created us to be and what He's called us to do. We don't have the time or the energy. Jesus said, "Woe to you when all men speak well of you" (Luke 6:26). If you're making everyone else happy—if everybody likes you—you probably aren't living to please God. Because women who are living to please God sometimes say no. They stand up for things (like truth and righteousness) and stand against things (like immorality and ungodliness and sin). Which doesn't make other people pleased.

Passivity: This strategy has two aspects. One is the personal, private aspect. The approach to life that says, "I'm afraid to do anything, so I will do nothing. I'll just be an outside observer, a spectator, watching from the sidelines in my own life." The other aspect is relational. If people pleasing is actively trying to make others happy, passivity is refusing to take action in order to make others happy. Avoiding conflict by appeasement. Giving into others' demands. It's the path of least resistance. Let the bullies have their way. We'll take it all lying down. Or hiding in a corner or curled up in a fetal position, hoping that eventually they'll just go away. Jesus told us not to harbor hatred in our hearts toward others, not to seek revenge or engage in retaliation. He did not tell us to become perpetual victims. Or to cower in fear. When bullies came after Him—or the people under His protection—He stood up to them. He challenged these bullies, He confronted them, He exposed them. Sometimes He anticipated their attacks and took evasive action;

other times He cleverly outwitted them. Sometimes He did what He needed to do, said what He needed to say, and then walked away. Let *them* be afraid.

Aggression: The opposite of passivity, this is a strategy (and a behavior) we don't usually connect with fear—or with women, frankly. But it's becoming more and more common. We scream, we shout, we threaten, we rail. We know that the louder and angrier we sound, the further back people will stand. Which is what we want. Because if they got close, they'd see how weak and powerless and out of control we feel—how totally frustrated and truly frightened we really are.

I more fear what is within me
than what comes from without.

—Martin Luther

Denial: If we can't see it, then it doesn't exist. If we don't acknowledge it, then it isn't real. If we pretend it never happened. If we refuse to hear. When we choose denial, we're trying to shield ourselves from a truth (or a lot of truths) we fear. And from the consequences of acknowledging the truth, from the responsibility of acting on it—which is often a scary prospect in and of itself. But the energy it takes to maintain the delusion is exhausting. And often the undercurrent of fear and dread is far worse than the truth would be, if we just faced it—which, sooner or later, we'll have to anyway. Even if the truth is every

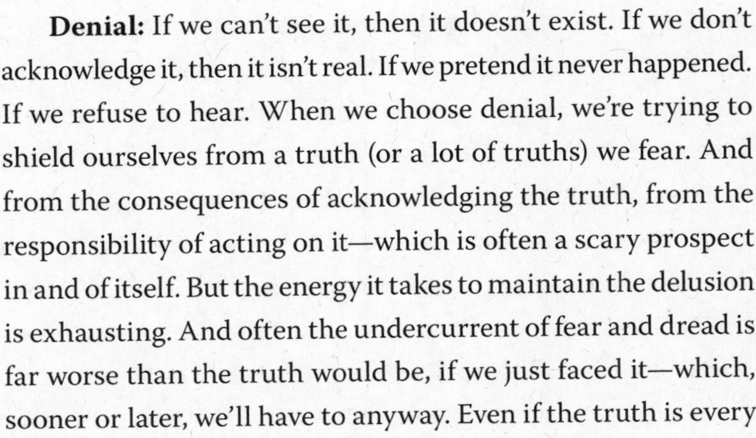

bit as awful as we feared, putting off facing it won't make it go away. It may allow it to grow much, much worse.

Self-sabotage: Some of us have a button we push when we believe things are going too well, when we're afraid that we're being set up for a big disappointment, a great letdown—eventually. When we're afraid that something will go wrong, because something always goes wrong, and we decide we can't live with the suspense, just waiting for it to happen. Or when we feel unworthy, undeserving. So we push that button. We start making poor choices, behaving in unhealthy, destructive, self-sabotaging ways. We think, if we go ahead and ruin it all now—if we lose it all now—then we won't have to be afraid of losing it later.

There are other coping mechanisms we use. Things we do to numb ourselves, to distract ourselves, to drown out the sounds of our fears. Things we do to build walls to protect ourselves and keep others at arm's length. Things we substitute for real relationships that are scarier and take much more hard work. Things like eating disorders, hoarding, compulsive shopping and spending, internet addiction, alcohol and drug abuse, pornography and sexual addictions.

Sometimes I find myself being obsessive about organization and preparation and planning—which is a problem when it's driven by fear. It's a problem when the underlying idea is that it's somehow within my power to anticipate and prevent every problem, protect myself from every crisis or disaster.

I can also be a little obsessive about acquiring information. I still remember the PSAs that ran during after-school specials when I was a child announcing, "Knowledge is power!"—by which they probably meant stay in school, not stay up until the wee hours of the morning researching every cause, every symptom, every treatment, every possible approach to dealing with . . . whatever it is that concerns me or someone I care about.

Trust the past to God's mercy, the present to God's love, and the future to God's providence.

—St. Augustine

For a long time, I forced myself to face my fears out of fear of living in fear.

(It's okay if you need to go back and read that sentence again. It doesn't make sense. But it took me a while to realize that myself.)

I used to make myself do a lot of things I didn't want to do—things I was pretty sure I wouldn't like, things that sure enough, I hated—because I was afraid that saying no meant I was giving in to fear. I was afraid saying no meant I'd miss out on a new adventure or a special experience. I'd already missed out on so many! I was also afraid that saying no would disappoint all the new friends I was making.

I thought I was facing my fears by forcing myself into new situations, new experiences, that were uncomfortable or unappealing to me. But I was only giving in to different fears—and letting them control me.

These days I do still take on new challenges and adventures, but only if I want to! Or if I clearly sense God leading me to. The rest of the time, I feel free to say, "No thanks! You go ahead. I'm sure it will be great. Have fun without me!" And I mean it. God has set me free from camping. I will never go back.

But you see how easy it is to get confused. To get all mixed up and twisted around and tied up in knots. There's just no way that in our own wisdom, in our own strength, in our own efforts, we can ever be free from fear. Our own strategies consistently fail us. They let us down time and time again. And our coping mechanisms only create problems—much worse problems—than the ones we had to begin with.

Our fears just grow stronger. Our worries grow greater. Our anxieties pile higher and higher. We can't just do nothing. We've got to do something. But what?

What is the right something? What is the right strategy? What is the right way to face and overcome our fear?

I think the first step, the first right something can be found tucked into a story in John 5:1–13. It's what you do right after you admit that you have a problem.

The Bible tells us that, when Jesus was in the city of Jerusalem, He stopped by the Pool of Bethesda. This pool was supposed to have healing powers. People believed that from time to time an angel would come and stir the waters, and the first person to get into the pool afterward would be healed.

All kinds of people who needed healing came to this pool—but especially the blind, the lame, the paralyzed. Those who couldn't really do anything else BUT sit and wait. And hope and pray. Apparently there was one man at the pool that day who had been paralyzed for thirty-eight years.

When the brilliant theologian and scholar Matthew Henry wrote his famous Bible commentary in 1704, he pointed out that thirty-eight years was a very long time for anyone to have to live in such pain and misery, such agony. Indeed, Henry observed, the man had suffered longer than most people lived in the 1700s, or in any previous century, including the one in which the poor man lay by the pool.[1] Yes, it had been a lifetime of suffering.

The Scriptures say that when Jesus saw the man and learned how long he had been that way, He asked him a surprising question:

> Do you want to get well? (John 5:6)

Wait a minute. What kind of a question is that? Isn't it obvious? Who wouldn't want to get well?

Actually a lot of people. It seems there are a lot of people in this world who would rather stay the way they are. They're familiar with their fears. They're comfortable with their pain. They've grown accustomed to their limitations. As miserable as they are, they're afraid of change.

It may be hard for an egg to turn into a bird:
it would be a jolly sight harder for it to learn to fly
while remaining an egg. We are like eggs at present.
And you cannot go on indefinitely being just an
ordinary, decent egg. We must be hatched or go bad.

—C. S. Lewis

The paralyzed man immediately began explaining why, all these times, he hadn't been able to get into the pool fast enough. He really did want to be healed. He was certain his healing would come from those waters, and he was so focused on them. So frustrated that all his attempts had been useless, his efforts thwarted. He didn't realize he was talking to the Great Physician.

> I am the Lord, who heals you. (Exod. 15:26)

After listening to the whole story, all the man's frustrations and complaints, Jesus simply said: "Get up! Pick up your mat and walk!" (John 5:8).

Just like that.

No mad dash for the pool. No scrambling, no scraping, no crawling, or clawing. No jostling or jockeying for position—no pushing anyone else or being pushed out of the way. No scheming, no plotting, no manipulating. No groveling. No pleading.

All he did was answer a question. It took some soul searching, but he did it.

And then Jesus took it from there.

So imagine you and I are sitting by the Pool of Bethesda today. We're so tired and frustrated, worn out and weary from our battles with worry and fear. Nothing we've tried has helped. None of our strategies, none of our efforts have worked. We're just failing and flailing all over the place. We're in so much pain.

Suddenly Jesus is standing before us, with a look of compassion and tenderness on His face. He asks a question:

"Do you want to get well?"

What will you say?

Bible Study

1. Read John 8:32. Spend a few moments in reflection and prayer. What are some of the strategies you've used to fight fear in the past—or that you've realized you're using right now?

- ☐ Manipulation or Control
- ☐ Aggression
- ☐ Denial
- ☐ People Pleasing
- ☐ Coping Mechanisms
- ☐ ________________
- ☐ Risk Avoidance
- ☐ Perfectionism
- ☐ Self-Sabotage
- ☐ Passivity
- ☐ Other ________________
- ☐ ________________

2. How have these strategies worked—or not worked—for you? (Try to think of some specific examples.) What's been the cost—or the consequence?

3. What did Jesus promise in John 8:36? What encouragement (and warning) do we find in Galatians 5:1?

4. We'll be talking more in depth about biblical strategies for facing fear in Chapter Six, but we've already mentioned quite a few principles and truths we can hold on to . . . and it's not likely that they're all new to you. What are some things you've learned you can do to walk in the freedom God has given you?

5. Turn to 2 Corinthians 12:7–10. Sometimes God allows us to do battle with "a thorn in [our] flesh." A particular area of weakness or vulnerability. According to Paul, what's the purpose of such a thorn? How does it serve us? What can we learn from it? How can we grow through it? What should our attitude be?

6. Choose one of the following verses (or one mentioned previously in the chapter) to memorize and meditate on this week:

John 8:12	Psalm 118:5
Jeremiah 17:14	Psalm 119:32
Ephesians 5:8–10	Isaiah 40:30–31

7. Take a few moments to record any further thoughts or reflections in your journal.

chapter four

Far Too Expensive

Worry does not empty tomorrow of its sorrow;
it empties today of its strength.

—Corrie Ten Boom

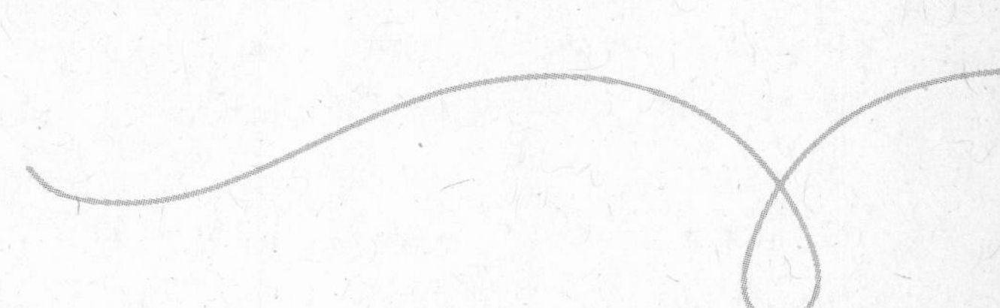

Years ago I ran across some fascinating statistics. Someone once conducted a lot of research and surveys, did some complicated in-depth analysis, and determined that of all the things we fear—of all the things we spend hours and hours worrying about:

40 percent will never happen
30 percent have already happened—things in the past you can't change or undo
12 percent are health related—ironic, since worry aggravates most health issues
10 percent are petty, random, miscellaneous

Leaving only 8 percent that are "legitimate" issues—which we'd have a lot more focus and energy and strength to address if we weren't wasting so much on all of the other ones![1]

Like so many other women, I constantly feel there are not enough hours in the day. There are so many things I have to do. And then the things I really want to do, for myself or others. Things I really believe are important. I just can't seem to find the time. Which is why I get really cranky when I'm stuck in pointless meetings, endless traffic, long lines, or even disappointing movies. Catch me afterward and you'll see me rolling my eyes in exasperation: "Well, that's two hours of my life I'll never get back!" Or quoting one of my favorite lines from the Pixar's *A Bug's Life*, where an inebriated housefly decides to leave right in the middle of a really bad circus performance: "I only got 24 hours to live and I ain't gonna waste it here!"

The point is that I know life is short. Time is precious. I don't want to waste a minute of it. But how much of my time have I wasted, how much of my life have I wasted—living in fear? Worrying about things that will never happen or have already happened. Things I have no control over. Or that don't really matter. How much time have I wasted being anxious and uptight and stressed?

Dozens of studies done more recently estimate that we Americans, Canadians, and British spend an average of two to three hours a day worrying *just about our jobs or our finances*. It adds up to fifteen to twenty hours a week, or approximately five years out of our lives.

That's a lot of time. Precious time. Time we can never get back.

And time isn't the only thing that fear and worry can cost us. Ask the Children of Israel.

The Old Testament tells us God miraculously delivered His people after hundreds of years of slavery in the land of Egypt. He led them through the Red Sea (another miracle) across the desert to a land that He had promised to give them, the same land He had told Abraham that His descendants would one day make their own.

There were already some pretty fierce people living there and they would have to be moved out. By force. But this was part of God's plan. He had pronounced judgment on these people long ago for the evil they had done. He allowed them to occupy the land until He was ready to bring His people into it. Now the time had come.

God was very clear about His will in this situation. He was very clear in His direction and instruction. Clear about the role He would play in the inevitable battles and what the outcome would be: "The LORD your God, who is going before you, will fight for you, as he did for you in Egypt, before your very eyes . . ." (Deut. 1:30).

Maybe you remember the story from Sunday school: Moses sent twelve spies, one from each tribe, to scout out the situation in advance.

> Go up through the Negev and on into the hill country. See what the land is like and whether the people who live there are strong or weak, few or many. What kind of land do they live in? Is it good or bad? What kind of towns do they live in? Are they unwalled or fortified? How is the soil? Is it fertile or poor? Are there trees in it or not? Do your best to bring back some of the fruit of the land. (Num. 13:17–20).

The men did just as Moses asked. They came back and reported to the whole Israelite community that the land was indeed good. They all agreed it was rich and fertile—"flowing with milk and honey." They had brought back some of its bountiful fruit for everyone to see.

However, the spies reported, the people already living in the land were large and powerful—not just in number but in physical size. They described them as being the descendants of a well-known race of giants. These "giants" had many fortified cities and strongholds.

Even so, the spy called Caleb said, "We should go up and take possession of the land, for we can certainly do it" (Num. 13:30). What difference did it matter how many there were or how big they were or how strong? God said He would take care of them. Let's go!

> But the men who had gone up with him said, "We can't attack those people; they are stronger than we are." And they spread among the Israelites a bad report about the land they had explored. They said, "The land we explored devours those living in it. All the people we saw there are of great size. . . . We seemed like grasshoppers in our own eyes, and we looked the same to them." (Num. 13:31–33)

The beginning of anxiety is the end of faith,
and the beginning of true faith is the end of anxiety.

—George Mueller

Throughout the day this bad report circulated among the people. They went back and forth, talking it over for hours on end. They tried to remember every horrible story about giants they'd ever heard. They let a lot of nasty images into their heads. Their imaginations were running wild, inventing all kinds of terrible scenarios for themselves and their loved ones. By nightfall, they had all gotten so worked up, they were weeping with fear. They cried out:

> If only we had died in Egypt! Or in this desert! Why is the LORD bringing us to this land only to let us fall by the sword? Our wives and children will be taken as plunder. Wouldn't it be better for us to go back to Egypt? (Num. 14:2–3)

Because . . . slavery was awesome? Being tortured and beaten and worked (literally) to death was better than trusting God?

The people let worry and fear drive every other thought from their mind. They couldn't remember who God really was (all they had learned about His nature and His character) or any of the amazing things He had done for them. They couldn't remember how awful their lives had been before He rescued them.

Moses was distraught. The two godly men he had sent, the two "good" spies, pleaded with the people once again:

> The land we passed through and explored is exceedingly good. If the LORD is pleased with us, he will lead us into that land . . . and will give it to us. Only

> do not rebel against the Lord. And do not be afraid of the people of the land, because we will swallow them up. Their protection is gone, but the Lord is with us. Do not be afraid of them. (Num. 14:7–9)

But the people chose to listen to their fear instead. And, because they listened to their fear, they chose to rebel against God. They chose to disobey Him. Their fear, their rebellion, and their disobedience cost them more than they could ever have imagined.

God could have destroyed them all—wiped them off the face of the earth and started over. (He thought about it.) Instead, He showed them mercy. He forgave them. But there were consequences. Brutally painful consequences.

Because they would not trust Him, because they would not go when He said, "Go!"—these people lost all of the wonderful blessings God had been preparing for them. They would have no home, no country of their own. They would never get to enter the Promised Land. Ever. At all.

No, they would be forced to wander in the desert for forty years—one year for each day the spies had explored Canaan—until every member of their generation had died (except Joshua and Caleb). Then, and only then, would their children inherit the precious Promised Land.

When the people realized what they had lost—when they learned what their worry and fear had cost them—they felt sick. And then they did an abrupt about-face. They changed their minds and decided they were not too scared to obey God after all. But it was too late. They tried to enter the Promised

Land on their own and they were soundly defeated in battle. There was nothing they could do now but return to the harsh desert, there to wander for forty long, miserable years.

It's true, God was with them, even then. Even then, in His love, in His mercy and grace, He led them every step of the way. He protected them. He provided for them.

But what a price they had to pay!

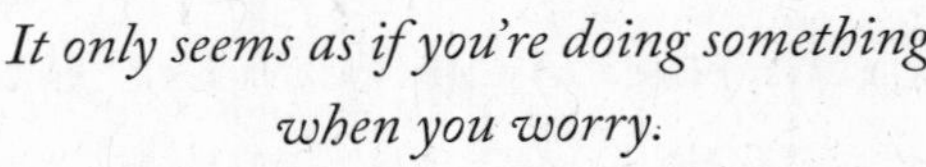

It only seems as if you're doing something when you worry.

—Lucy Maud Montgomery

Maybe we should take a closer look at what our worry and fear could cost us today.

Physically: Fear, worry, stress—these emotions have been shown to have a devastating effect on our health. They can physically make us sick or aggravate other health issues such as high blood pressure, heart palpitations, heart attacks, heart disease, nausea, dizziness, sweating, dry mouth, headaches, muscle aches and/or tension, fatigue, insomnia, skin conditions, digestive disorders, impaired bone growth, infertility, hormonal imbalances, asthma, arthritis, diabetes. In addition, worry is famous (or should that be infamous?) for compromising our immune system—making us more vulnerable to other sicknesses and diseases. Obviously there are some health issues and physical challenges we have no control over. But clearly there are some symptoms—some complications—we don't have to pile on. There are some we can avoid, reduce, or eliminate by choosing not to worry but to trust God and take Him at his Word.

Mentally and emotionally: Just from a medical perspective, living in a constant state of anxiety, worry, or fear can cause all kinds of irritability and frustration, mood swings, depression, and decreased mental function. If that last one caught your attention, it should. Worry can lead to a lot of loss. Loss of memory, loss of perspective, loss of rationality, loss of ability to concentrate, loss of ability to think clearly, prioritize, and make wise decisions. Loss of ability to differentiate facts from feelings. In the Old Testament, confusion was a weapon God often used to destroy the wicked. It's not what He wants for His beloved children (1 Cor. 14:33).

Spiritually: Worry and fear rob us of the sweetness we are meant to experience in our relationship with God. The hope and peace and strength and comfort He gives. We lose sight of who He is and what He has done for us. We lose the joy of our salvation. We don't experience the abundant life He has called us to. We become miserable and unhappy. We feel guilty and ashamed. As the Children of Israel discovered, fear and worry often lead to rebellion and disobedience. Which leads to more guilt and shame.

Practically: Every day we make thousands of choices. Practical choices. What we'll eat and drink, what we'll wear. Where we'll go. What we'll do. What we'll say. How we'll respond to specific challenges, distractions, temptations, responsibilities, and opportunities. How we won't. We can make all of those choices from a place of faith and trust, a place of courage and confidence. Led by the Spirit of God, walking in His light. Or we can make those choices out of fear and worry and doubt. Stumbling around in the darkness. Going from bad to worse.

Relationally: Fear robs us of the blessings and benefits of community. It keeps us from experiencing the "iron sharpening iron" effect (Prov. 27:17), from encouraging one another and building each other up (1 Thess. 5:10, Eph. 4:29). It damages or even destroys what could otherwise be strong, healthy, happy, Christ-honoring relationships with family and friends. For instance, we can be too afraid to open our hearts to others, keeping them at arm's length. Or so afraid of losing them that we behave in very unhealthy ways. If we choose to be fearful and anxious all the time, we'll lose friends who could otherwise be a blessing to us but need to keep their distance, for their own peace of mind! Then again, we may end up being responsible for dragging others down with us to our unhealthy, unhappy place. Instead of strengthening each other, we end up poisoning each other. Like the Children of Israel did. Spreading doubt and fear instead of courage, hope, and faith.

This is hardly an exhaustive list—just a brief overview of some of the most basic, most obvious costs. If each one of us could see our own itemized bill—if we only knew all that our fear and worry had cost us, day after day, year after year—we might take more seriously the biblical admonitions: Do NOT worry. Do NOT fear.

You know, God had good reasons—*has* good reasons—for repeating those words hundreds of times in Scripture. He loves us. He wants what's best for us. And what's best for us is not to be consumed with worry. Not to live in fear.

Beloved, I say, let your fears go, lest they make you fainthearted. Stop inspiring fear in those around you and now take your stand in faith. God has been good and He will continue to manifest His goodness. . . . Let us approach these days expecting to see the goodness of the Lord manifest. Let us be strong and of good courage, for the Lord will fight for us if we stand in faith.

—Francis Frangipane

Maybe you've noticed that, up to this point, I've taken care to say that fear and worry *can lead* to sin. They can *cause* us to sin. But *are* they sins, in and of themselves? Is fear a sin? Is worry a sin?

Some people say that if God says, "Do not," and you do, then it's a sin—simple as that. But I think that definition might be a little too simple. It overlooks or ignores some pretty significant distinctions, like the differences between worry and fear. And the difference in Scripture between a command (an order), an exhortation (a word meant to urge strongly, to warn, or advise), and a word intended to offer comfort or reassurance.*

*I don't think we should forget that there are also medical conditions (such as hypoglycemia) and prescription drugs known to trigger symptoms of anxiety, which have nothing to do with our true mental, emotional, or spiritual state. The last thing we want to do is foist guilt and condemnation on someone whose "sin" is suffering from low blood sugar!

Personally, I believe worry is a sin—because it's a choice. Choosing to dwell on our doubts and fears, our anxious thoughts (Rom. 14:23). Engaging in what the Bible describes as "vain imagination" or "futile thinking" or pointless speculation. (Rom. 1:21, 2 Cor. 10:5)

The word "worry" comes from the Old English word *wyrgan*, which means "to strangle." Later it became *worien*, which means to use your teeth to grab another creature by the throat—and kill it by shaking it to death. (Picture a wild dog or a wolf that's caught hold of a sheep or some other small animal—they "worry" it to death.) When we worry, that's what we do. We deliberately ignore God's admonishment to take every thought captive (2 Cor. 10:5), NOT to be anxious but to trust Him and to think on things that are true and right and lovely and pure (Phil. 4:6–8). Instead, we latch on to a negative thought or a bunch of negative thoughts. We grab them with our teeth and refuse to let go of them. We churn. We toss and turn. We shake them this way and that. From a distance it looks like we're strangling them. But the truth is they're strangling us.

Fear, however, is a little more complicated. Because—as we discussed earlier—there is such a thing as healthy fear. Reverent fear. Fear can be a biological response to real and present danger, the "fight-or-flight" response that God designed to help keep us alive. And sometimes, I believe fear is an affliction—a kind of torment, a kind of suffering. A trial, a test of our faith.

Maybe the best way to put it is that *feeling* fear is not a sin any more than feeling tempted is. But *giving in* to it . . . that's a different matter.

I do think (considering all that Scripture teaches on the subject) that giving in to fear is a sin. Making allowances for it. Making excuses for it. I think feeding fear is a sin, nurturing fear and causing it to grow. Giving fear a place in your heart and life, letting it take control of you, letting it rule over you—these things are sins. Surrendering to fear, instead of resisting it, fighting it—crying out to God for His help and deliverance.

Sometimes fear, too, is a choice. Sometimes it is a sin. And when it is, we need to repent of it.

Even so, Romans 8:1 says, "There is no condemnation for those who belong to Christ Jesus" (NLT). Only the constant, loving encouragement of our Heavenly Father to listen to Him and let Him help us choose what is better.

It reminds me of a story I once read in *Streams in the Desert*:

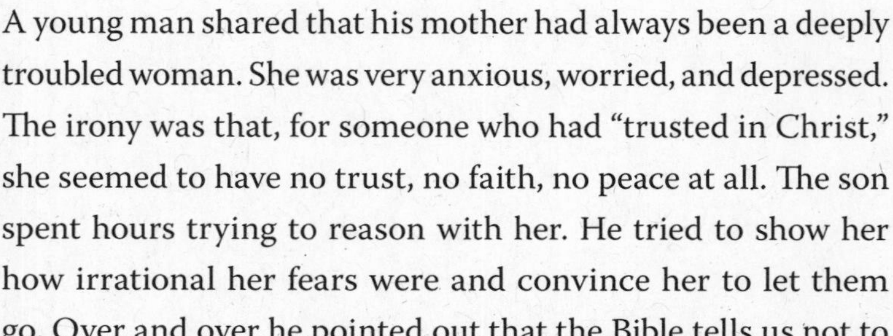

People become attached to their burdens sometimes more than the burdens are attached to them.

—George Bernard Shaw

A young man shared that his mother had always been a deeply troubled woman. She was very anxious, worried, and depressed. The irony was that, for someone who had "trusted in Christ," she seemed to have no trust, no faith, no peace at all. The son spent hours trying to reason with her. He tried to show her how irrational her fears were and convince her to let them go. Over and over he pointed out that the Bible tells us not to worry—that worry only robs us of the joy and peace that could be ours. All to no avail.

Then one day, he saw something that astonished him. His mother met him that morning with a huge smile on her face. All the worry and fear was gone. Amazed, he asked what had happened to her. She began telling him about a dream she had the night before:

> . . . In her dream, she was walking along a highway with a large crowd of people, all of whom seemed very tired and burdened. The people were all carrying little black bundles, and she noticed that more bundles were being dropped along the way by numerous repulsive-looking creatures that seemed quite demonic in nature. As the bundles were dropped, the people stooped to pick them up and carry them.
>
> Like everyone else in her dream, she also carried her needless load, being weighted down with the Devil's bundles. After a while, she looked up and saw a Man whose face was love and bright as He moved through the crowd, comforting the people. Finally He came to her, and she realized it was her Savior. She looked at Him, telling Him how tired she was, and He smiled sadly and said, "My dear child, these bundles you carry are not from Me, and you have no need of them. They are the Devil's burdens, and they are wearing out your life. You need to drop them and

> simply refuse to touch them with even one of your fingers. Then you will find your path easy, and you will feel as if I carried you on eagles' wings." (Exodus 19:4)
>
> The Savior touched her hand, and peace and joy quickly filled her soul. As she saw herself in her dream casting her burdens to the ground and ready to throw herself at His feet in joyful thanksgiving, she suddenly awoke, finding that all her worries were gone.[2]

I believe we have a choice. We can choose to pick up those bundles—we can choose to carry those burdens, to be weighed down by worry and fear. We can give in to despair. Or we can listen to our Savior when He says, "These things are not from Me." We can let them go. We can choose to leave our burdens at His feet.

We can choose to have faith, choose to believe, choose to be free.

Bible Study

1. What has fear or worry cost you? Can you be specific? Think of examples from your own life—mistakes made, opportunities lost, the drama or trauma you've suffered.

2. What has fear or worry given you in return?

3. Look up Matthew 6:25–34. You may want to underline key words or phrases in your Bible. Then answer the following questions:

   a) What kinds of things does Jesus tell us NOT to worry about?

b) Why not?

c) What should we focus on instead? (v. 33)

4. Read Matthew 11:28–30. How does Jesus describe Himself? What does He offer us?

Something to think about: In this word picture, Jesus isn't the farmer driving the team—He's the other ox. The older, wiser, more experienced ox, paired with the young ox (us). He is the one who knows the path, takes the lead, and sets the pace. All we have to do is keep in step, stay connected, and follow His lead.

5. What "bundles" or burdens are you most tempted to pick up—to try to carry on your own—today? Make a list and then offer each one to Jesus. Promise Him that you will leave them in His care.

If it helps you remember, draw a little bundle shape around each one in your journal or on a separate piece of paper that you tape to your desk or refrigerator. Or tie up a little cloth "bundle" and put it where you'll see it often as a reminder not to keep picking these burdens up. Let Him take care of them.

6. Choose one of the following verses (or one mentioned previously in the chapter) to memorize and meditate on this week:

Joshua 1:9	Psalm 27:14
Philippians 4:6	Lamentations 3:22–23
1 Peter 5:7	Psalm 29:11

7. Take a few moments to record any further thoughts or reflections in your journal.

chapter five

Fear Not!

Courage is fear that has said its prayers.

—Dorothy Bernard

The elderly woman had been bedbound for eighteen years with chronic illness—she lived in constant pain. Her husband and caregiver had become ill as well. He needed a wheelchair to get around the house. Day after day, week after week, year after year, the couple wrestled with their ever-increasing physical limitations and all the associated frustrations and complications. If they had grown depressed or discouraged, if they had felt angry or bitter, if they had been anxious and fearful or worried about the future—well, it would have been understandable. No one would have blamed them. But this couple shared such a sweet spirit, such joy and peace, that visitors to their home couldn't help but be challenged, convicted, and inspired.

One such visitor, Civilla Martin, felt compelled to ask the couple for their secret. How could they be so content, so at peace, with all the trials they faced? The elderly woman responded with a reference to Scripture, Matthew 10:29–31. She said simply, "His eye is on the sparrow."

Deeply moved, Civilla Martin went home and penned these words:

> Why should I feel discouraged, why should the shadows come, Why should my heart be lonely, and long for heaven and home, When Jesus is my portion? My constant friend is He: His eye is on the sparrow, and I know He watches me;
>
> "Let not your heart be troubled," His tender word I hear, And resting on His goodness, I lose my doubts and fears; Though by the path He leadeth, but one step I may see; His eye is on the sparrow, and I know He watches me;
>
> Whenever I am tempted, whenever clouds arise, When songs give place to sighing, when hope within me dies, I draw the closer to Him, from care He sets me free; His eye is on the sparrow, and I know He watches me.

We don't have to live bound by worry or fear—because of Jesus. Because of who He is and what we mean to Him.

When you really believe in God, it gives you a courage, a confidence that enables you to meet the things coming.

—Della Reese

In John 14:27, Jesus said, "Peace I leave with you; my peace I give you. I do not give to you as the world gives. Do not let your hearts be troubled and do not be afraid."

But for these words to mean anything to us, we have to know who Jesus is—I mean really know and understand who He is.

> Who is this King of glory?
> The LORD strong and mighty. (Ps 24:8)

The Centurion knew. Of all people, he understood—more than most. Better even than some of Jesus' disciples did. Although he was a Gentile (a non-Jew) and a Roman (from the nation occupying and oppressing Israel), he dared risk the scorn of his own people and the scorn of the Jewish people by reaching out to a rabbi for help. He had a desperate need. His beloved servant was sick and at the point of death.

This centurion was apparently an extraordinary man, because the Jews in his own community had come to respect him and were willing to approach Jesus on his behalf. Jesus was actually on the way to the Centurion's house, when the man sent a messenger to stop Him:

> Lord, don't trouble yourself, for I do not deserve to have you come under my roof. That is why I did not even consider myself worthy to come to you. But say the word, and my servant will be healed. For I myself am a man under authority, with soldiers under me. I tell this one, "Go," and he goes; and that one "Come,"

> and he comes. I say to my servant, "Do this," and he does it. (Luke 7:6–8)

Let's pause the story here for just a moment and compare what the Centurion declared about Jesus to the words of the father of a demon-possessed boy in Mark 9:22–24.

This other man brought his son to Jesus and said, "If you can do anything, take pity on us and help us."

Jesus answered by repeating the man's words: "'If you can'?"

You're asking Me IF I can do something? You mean, you don't think I can? Then it's not really a question of what I can do, is it? If you don't know who I am, if you don't believe who I am, if you don't trust Me, how can I possibly help you?

Then Jesus said gently, "Everything is possible for him who believes."

God knows we've all had moments when we've been weary and exhausted and at the end of our strength, when we've come to Him with little hope, little faith that He could or would do anything for us. More than once I've prayed a faithless prayer, only to hear Jesus whisper to my heart, "*If* I can?" And in tears of repentance, I've cried along with the boy's father: "Lord, I do believe; help me overcome my unbelief!"

The Centurion, however, knew who Jesus was. Believed who He was. And not only believed—he recognized that Jesus had been given authority by God the Father. Whatever Jesus commanded would be done, whether He was there personally or not. It wasn't what Jesus physically did or said that brought healing. It was the authority He had.

Jesus Himself said, "All authority in heaven and on earth has been given to me" (Matt. 28:18).

The natural world submitted to His authority: the wind and the waves obeyed Him. The fig tree withered and died at His command. In the physical realm, Jesus exercised authority over sickness and disease. He healed the blind, the lame, the deaf. The spirit world acknowledged Him—demons trembled in His presence and begged Him not to torture them.

Jesus had the power to read people's thoughts and reveal their hearts. He had the authority to forgive sin. Jesus had control of His own destiny. He said, "No one can take my life from me. I sacrifice it voluntarily" (John 10:18 NLT). He had authority over death and hell—it couldn't keep Him in the grave. He rose from the dead in power and glory. Now He's seated at the right hand of the Father, the King of Kings and the Lord of Lords.

He says that if we invite Him, He'll come and make His home in our hearts (John 14:23). His Spirit will live in us and through us. He will constantly watch over us, protect us, and provide for us. He will comfort us and strengthen us and sustain us. He will bless us in ways we can't even begin to imagine.

Jesus promised his disciples three things—
that they would be completely fearless,
absurdly happy, and in constant trouble.

—G. K. Chesterton

Romans 8:28–30 tells us, "And we know that God causes everything to work together for the good of those who love God and are called according to his purpose for them. For God knew his people in advance, and he chose them to become like his Son, so that his Son would be the firstborn among many brothers and sisters. And having chosen them, he called them to come to him. And having called them, he gave them right standing with himself. And having given them right standing, he gave them his glory" (NLT).

This verse has both comforted and challenged believers for centuries. What exactly does it mean, God causes *everything* (or "all things") to work together for *good*? Looking back, we've experienced some pretty unhappy things. Heart-breaking things. Evil things. There are shameful things we've done and shameful things that have been done to us. It's these very things—these kinds of experiences—that make us afraid to trust God with the future.

Can things that make no earthly sense somehow have heavenly purpose and meaning? How is this possible?

The answer lies in the sovereignty of God. According to the dictionary, the word "sovereignty" means having supreme, unlimited power or authority, complete control. To be sovereign is to be preeminent; indisputable; greatest in degree; utmost or extreme; above all others in character, importance, and excellence.

Colossians 1:15–18 says that Jesus "is the image of the invisible God, the firstborn over all creation. For by him all things were created: things in heaven and on earth. . . . He is before all things, and in him all things hold together. And he is the head of the body, the church; he is the beginning and the firstborn . . . so that in everything he might have the supremacy."

Because Jesus is all of these things, although evil is prevalent and we live in a fallen world, He has the power and the authority and the ability to cause all things to work together for our good—just as it says in Romans 8:28–30. He can overrule the enemy of our souls. He can override the intentions of others, overcome our limitations, and bring something beautiful out of something ugly and scarred.

Remember that, when God talks about our good, He doesn't just mean our immediate comfort or happiness. He means that He is making us more and more like Jesus, which will ultimately give us the greatest joy now and in eternity.

Author, preacher, and Bible teacher John Piper points out that God was able to take the most "spectacular" sin (the greatest evil, the most wicked injustice) in the history of the world—the crucifixion of Jesus—and use it to triumph over the devil, redeem God's children, and glorify His Son.[1]

> When you were dead in your sins . . . God made you alive with Christ. He forgave us all our sins, having canceled the written code, with its regulations, that was against us and that stood opposed to us; he took it away, nailing it to the cross. And having disarmed the powers and authorities, he made a public spectacle of them, triumphing over them by the cross. (Col. 2:13–15)

The metaphor here suggests a victorious general leading his captives—the physical evidence of His complete and total victory—through the streets for all the people to see.

It's a powerful reminder that God and the devil are not equals. The devil is a created being and, more than that, a defeated foe. His eternal destiny has already been determined. First John 4:4 tells us, "Greater is he that is in you than he that is in the world" (ASV).

Believe it or not, this almighty power, this absolute authority, this supreme sovereignty of God is just one reason for His children to fear not! There are others . . .

How sweet the name of Jesus sounds
in a believer's ear! It soothes his sorrows, heals his
wounds, and drives away his fear.

—John Newton

Fear not, for I have redeemed you;
I have summoned you by name; you are mine.
When you pass through the waters,
I will be with you;
and when you pass through the rivers,
they will not sweep over you.
When you walk through the fire,
you will not be burned;
the flames will not set you ablaze.

> For I am the LORD, your God,
> the Holy One of Israel, your Savior. (Isa. 43:1–3)

God says we are His—we belong to Him. He loves us truly. Deeply. Intimately. Completely. In Scripture He uses some of the most beautiful imagery, the most poetic language to describe how He feels about us and the relationship He longs to have with us. The relationship He created us to share.

Sometimes He compares Himself to a bridegroom rejoicing over us, His beloved bride (Hos. 2:19–20; Eph. 5:22–23). Other times He pictures Himself as a father carrying his little son (Deut. 1:31) or as a mother comforting her child (Isa. 66:13). Jesus is referred to as our "older brother" (Col. 1:18, Heb. 2:10–18) and our dearest friend. Most of us can connect with at least one of these images. We can relate the love that we feel in our hearts for others (and ideally the love we've received from others) to get just a tiny sense of the kind of love God has for us. But, even if our human relationships fail to live up to God's example, as He intended them to, His love remains.

Isaiah 49:14–16 tells us,

> Zion said, "The LORD has forsaken me,
> the LORD has forgotten me."

But God answered,

> "Can a mother forget the baby at her breast
> and have no compassion on the child she has
> borne?"

Of course not!

Well, not normally. It *is* possible . . . but even if something as precious, as deep, as enduring as a mother's love fails, God's love will never fail.

God says,

> "Though she may forget,
> I will not forget you!
> See, I have engraved you on the palms of my hands."

I have engraved you on the palms of my hands.

Some translations of this Scripture say "inscribed," "tattooed," or "indelibly imprinted." What a powerful picture! We are never out of God's sight. Never out of His mind. Always in His thoughts. Always on His heart, under His wings—where we find refuge (Ps. 91:4).

In Ephesians 3:17b–18, Paul writes, "And I pray that you, being rooted and established in love, may have power, together with all the saints, to grasp how wide and long and high and deep is the love of Christ."

He goes on to say he wants us to "know" the love God has for us, to really grasp this life-transforming truth. The kind of knowing he prays for isn't just "head knowledge"—an intellectual assent to an established fact. It's "heart knowledge"—an ever-expanding, deepening, growing comprehension of a reality that cannot be fully understood apart from the supernatural intervention of God.

> [That you may really come] to know [practically, through experience for yourselves] the love of Christ, which far surpasses mere knowledge [without experience]; that you may be filled [through all your being] unto all the fullness of God [may have the richest measure of the divine Presence, and become a body wholly filled and flooded with God Himself]! (Eph. 3:19 AMP)

Then there's no room for fear! Not an inch.

In Romans 8:31–34, Paul asked,

> What shall we say about such wonderful things as these? If God is for us, who can ever be against us? Since he did not spare even his own Son but gave him up for us all, won't he also give us everything else? Who dares accuse us whom God has chosen for his own? No one—for God himself has given us right standing with himself. Who then will condemn us? No one—for Christ Jesus died for us and was raised to life for us, and he is sitting in the place of honor at God's right hand, pleading for us. (NLT)

When we know who Jesus is and what He did for us, how He loved us, how He died for us—when we know that our sins are forgiven, that our future is in Heaven, that even now Jesus Himself is praying for us, interceding on our behalf—how can we be afraid?

Paul continues, "Can anything ever separate us from Christ's love? Does it mean he no longer loves us if we have trouble or calamity, or are persecuted, or hungry, or destitute, or in danger, or threatened with death? . . . No, despite all these things, overwhelming victory is ours through Christ, who loved us."

He concludes, "I am convinced that nothing can ever separate us from God's love. Neither death nor life, neither angels nor demons, *neither our fears for today nor our worries about tomorrow*—not even the powers of hell can separate us from God's love. No power in the sky above or in the earth below—indeed, nothing in all creation will ever be able to separate us from the love of God that is revealed in Christ Jesus our Lord" (Rom. 8:35, 37–39 NLT, emphasis mine).

We can walk without fear, full of hope and courage and strength to do His will, waiting for the endless good which He is always giving as fast as He can get us able to take it in.

—George MacDonald

Corrie was only six years old when she first began to understand the reality of suffering and death. Her mother had taken her along on a visit to the home of a neighbor who had just lost a child to illness. Corrie would never forget the grief-stricken faces of the family gathered there. For the first time it occurred to the little girl that the members of *her* family—her brothers and sisters, her parents—could die. She was so distressed that she couldn't eat the rest of the day. And that night she couldn't fall asleep. When her father came in to check on her, she burst into tears.

"I need you," Corrie sobbed. "You can't die. You can't." Corrie's father sat down beside her and wisely resisted the urge to make a promise he couldn't keep. Instead, he said gently, "Corrie, when you and I go to Amsterdam, when do I give you your ticket?"

Surprised by the question, Corrie thought for a moment: "Why, just before we get on the train!"

"Exactly," said her father. "Our wise Father in heaven knows when we're going to need things, too. Don't run out ahead of Him, Corrie. When the time comes that some of us will have to die, you will look into your heart and find the strength you need—just in time."[2]

He was right. That strength did come to Corrie decades later, when she and her father and sister Betsie were arrested for hiding Jews in their home during the Nazi occupation of Holland. Just in time, God gave Corrie the strength that would sustain her through the indescribable horrors of the concentration camps and the brutal deaths of her beloved father and sister. It was this supernatural measure of grace and strength that then empowered her, as an elderly woman, to travel all over the world sharing her experience, preaching the gospel to millions of people, and proclaiming the truth that "there is no pit so deep, that the love of God is not deeper still."

We don't have to live in fear of what the future holds or how we will face the challenges that lie ahead. God is in control. We can bring all of our worries and fears to Him—and He will fill our hearts with His peace. For we have His assurance that, no matter what happens, He will always be with us. He loves us so much!

And we will find, as Corrie did, that He will give us all the strength and courage we need—right when we need it.

Have courage for the great sorrows of life and patience for the small ones; and when you have laboriously accomplished your daily task, go to sleep in peace. God is awake.

—Victor Hugo

Bible Study

1. Look up Isaiah 61:1–3 and then Isaiah 42:3. What do these verses (which speak prophetically of Jesus) reveal about God's heart toward us? What has He promised us?

2. According to Psalm 103:11–14, we don't have to live weighed down by guilt, bound by fear, or covered in shame. Why not?

3. What encouragement do we find in Hebrews 4:15–16?

4. Turn to 1 John 3:18–20. None of us is perfect, but when we are trying to do the right thing—trying to trust God and walk in obedience to His Word—we can "set our hearts at rest in his presence." How? Why?

5. Right now, pause for a few moments to reflect on who God is. How would you describe Him to someone who didn't know Him? List some of His names from Scripture, some of His attributes, some of the things He has done for you.

Now reflect on who you are to Him—what He says you mean to Him, how He describes His feelings toward you.

When your fears and worries threaten to fill your thoughts today, come back to these thoughts and choose to dwell on them instead.

6. Choose one of the following verses (or one mentioned previously in the chapter) to memorize or meditate on this week:

1 John 1:9–10	Psalm 56:3
Zephaniah 3:17	Psalm 32:7
Isaiah 12:2	Psalm 4:8

7. Take a few moments to record any further thoughts or reflections.

chapter six

Forget Not!

A little kingdom I possess,
where thoughts and feelings dwell;
and very hard the task I find of governing it well.

—Louisa May Alcott

When God calls us to face our fears—and overcome them—He promises to give us the strength we need. The courage we need. The wisdom and direction.

He's already give us the weapons—the battle strategies (2 Cor. 6:7, 2 Pet. 1:3) We find them described in detail, illustrated with real-life example after real-life example, in the pages of His Word.

It's time to take a closer look:

1. Remember. Remember who God is. Remember what He has done for us—how He has been with us and for us, working in us and through us. How He has protected and provided for us. How He has comforted us and strengthened us. All the things He has seen us through.

> Praise the LORD, O my soul;
>   all my inmost being, praise his holy name.
> Praise the LORD, O my soul,
>   and forget not all his benefits—
> who forgives all your sins
>   and heals all your diseases,

> who redeems your life from the pit
> and crowns you with love and compassion,
> who satisfies your desires with good things.
> (Ps. 103:1–5)

Remember all the things He has done for our friends and family, our church, our community. Our country. All the things He has done through the ages, in the lives of men and women in history, in Scripture.

> I will remember the deeds of the LORD;
> yes, I will remember your miracles of long ago.
> I will meditate on all your works
> and consider all your mighty deeds. . . .
> You are the God who performs miracles;
> you display your power among the peoples.
> (Ps. 77:11–12, 14)

As Joshua led the Children of Israel into the Promised Land, God did many amazing and wondrous things to demonstrate His power and love—to show them that He was with them. He would bless them in the new land. When the people arrived at the banks of the Jordan River, it was harvest time and the river was at its fullest. But as the priests carrying the Ark of the Covenant stepped into the water at the river's edge, the flow of water miraculously ceased. It was cut off upstream, and all the people were able to walk across the riverbed as if it were dry land.

While the priests stood there, Joshua sent the leaders of the Twelve Tribes back to the riverbed, commanding each of them to gather a large stone. "We will use these stones to build a memorial," he said. "In the future your children will ask you, 'What do these stones mean?' Then you can tell them, 'They remind us that the Jordan River stopped flowing when the Ark of the LORD's Covenant went across.' These stones will stand as a memorial among the people of Israel forever" (Josh. 4:6–7 NLT).

A memorial is a way to remember something precious or sacred, something historic, something vitally important. It's a wonderful tradition each of us can carry on in our own hearts, and with our own families. And a fabulous weapon against worry and doubt and fear.

If you haven't already, start building memorials to help you remember who God is and what He has done for you. Use a journal or a scrapbook, your blog or Facebook page or a smartphone app to count your blessings and recount specific memories, specific events, in which God touched your heart or life. Take pictures. Write down details. Or record them. Make videos or slideshows. Create a visual representation you can keep in front of you, like a jar of colorful stones, each one with a significant date written on it. Whatever you do, make sure you share them with others. Use your "memorials" to encourage and inspire not only your own heart but the hearts of those around you!

But as for me, I will always have hope;
I will praise you more and more.
My mouth will tell of your righteousness,
of your salvation all day long,
though I know not its measure.
I will come and proclaim your mighty acts, O Sovereign LORD;
I will proclaim your righteousness, yours alone.
Since my youth, O God, you have taught me,
and to this day I declare your marvelous deeds.
Even when I am old and gray,
do not forsake me, O God,
till I declare your power to the next generation,
your might to all who are to come.
(Ps. 71:14–18)

2. Resist. Resist the enemy of your soul (James 4:7, 1 Pet. 5:9). Resist the father of lies. Don't mindlessly embrace every anxious thought, every doubt, every fear that comes into your head. In *The Silver Chair* by C. S. Lewis, two children and a Marsh Wiggle named Puddleglum are held captive—spellbound—by an evil enchantress masquerading as an angel of light. She tries to discourage them and distract them from continuing on a desperate quest to rescue a long lost prince (a prince she herself has kidnapped and enslaved) by oh-so-sweetly insisting that no such prince exists. That in fact, everything they believe in and are fighting for is a lie . . . a fairy tale . . . a figment of their imagination.

Her gentle ridicule and cunning logic has them reeling, until Puddleglum takes a stand. He agrees that he's no match for the woman's clever arguments; he may be every bit as ignorant and foolish as she says. But, he says, "I'm on Aslan's side, even if there isn't any Aslan . . . and I'm going to live like a Narnian, even if there isn't any Narnia!" Though it takes tremendous effort, Puddleglum resists the enchantment and stubbornly clings to what he knows deep down is true. Suddenly the spell is broken. The witch's lies sound hollow and empty and powerless. The light of truth shines through.

Satan tries to convince us that everything we believe in is a lie, that we're foolish to have faith in Jesus. If we listen long enough to his nonsense, we'll soon find ourselves doubting everything we know to be true—including our own very real and powerful experience.

It's not a new strategy. He tried it on Jesus' disciples two thousand years ago. The world and Satan mocked them, too. Peter replied, "We did not follow cleverly invented stories when we told you about the power and coming of our Lord Jesus Christ, but we were eyewitnesses of his majesty" (2 Pet. 1:16). In other words, "We were there. We saw it happen. We experienced it. We know it's true!"

The Apostle Paul said, "I know the one in whom I trust, and I am sure that he is able to guard what I have entrusted to him until the day of his return" (2 Tim. 1:12 NLT).

So "take every thought captive," instead of letting your thoughts take control of you (2 Cor. 10:5).

> *We must be watchful, especially in the beginning of the temptation, for the enemy is more easily overcome in the beginning if he is not allowed to enter the door of our hearts, but is resisted outside the gate at his first knock.*
>
> —Thomas à Kempis

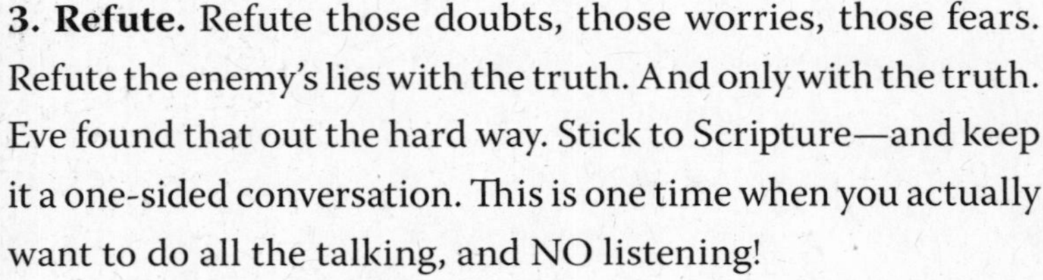

3. Refute. Refute those doubts, those worries, those fears. Refute the enemy's lies with the truth. And only with the truth. Eve found that out the hard way. Stick to Scripture—and keep it a one-sided conversation. This is one time when you actually want to do all the talking, and NO listening!

In Matthew 4, Jesus models for us how we should handle confrontation with the enemy of our souls. "Jesus was led by the Spirit into the desert to be tempted by the devil" (Matt. 4:1). Three times, Satan came to Him and challenged Him—tested Him—tempted Him to sin. There are probably any number of ways Jesus could have vanquished him supernaturally. He was, after all, God in the flesh. But Jesus didn't use His divine power to defeat the devil—perhaps because you and I are not God and we don't have that kind of power.

Instead, Jesus used a weapon that is at the disposal of every believer—from the newest "baby" Christian to the most seasoned saint. Every time the devil tempted him, Jesus answered: "IT IS WRITTEN . . ." (Matt. 4:4, 7, 10). He quoted Scripture. He used the Word of God, which is powerful and living, "sharper than any two-edged sword" (Heb. 4:12). He rebuked the father of lies with the Word of Truth. By His own example, Jesus showed us how to defeat the devil when he comes at us today.

So read the Scripture. Memorize it. Meditate on it. Think about it, reflect on what it means and how it applies to your life. Listen to it in the car or on the treadmill or as you fall asleep at night. Make a point of learning how to skillfully handle this powerful weapon of truth (2 Tim. 2:15)!

4. Guard your heart and renew your mind. Some of you have been wondering when I was going to get to this Scripture! Here it is: "Do not be anxious about anything, but in everything, by prayer and petition, with thanksgiving, present your requests to God. And the peace of God, which transcends all understanding, will guard your hearts and your minds in Christ Jesus" (Phil. 4:6–7).

Bring all of your needs to God, thanking Him that He is already at work meeting your needs, answering your prayers. Let His peace protect you.

In the Amplified Bible, Isaiah 26:3 says—speaking of God—"You will guard him *and* keep him in perfect *and* constant peace whose mind [both its inclination and its character] is stayed on You, because he commits himself to You, leans on You, *and* hopes confidently in You."

The New Living Translation puts it a little more simply:

> You will keep in perfect peace
> all who trust in you,
> all whose thoughts are fixed on you!

Keeping our thoughts fixed on Him is key. Ask Peter. He discovered he could walk on water, when he looked into the eyes of Jesus. But then he looked at the wind blowing and the waves crashing all around him, and fear and doubt started to sink him (Matt. 14:25–33). Just like they threaten to sink us. That's why we've got to stay focused on Jesus, and fix our eyes on Him (Heb. 12:1–3).

> Finally, brothers, whatever is true, whatever is noble, whatever is right, whatever is pure, whatever is lovely, whatever is admirable—if anything is excellent or praiseworthy—think about such things. (Phil. 4:8)

We've got to fill our hearts and minds with the truth, with positive, encouraging, uplifting things. But we also have to keep bad things out. We've got to be vigilant, to guard our hearts and minds against unhealthy or negative influences. They may be internal—thoughts we're tempted to dwell on, feelings we're tempted to wallow in. Or external—things we read and watch and listen to that only feed our fears and frustrations. Things that worry or depress and discourage us. Sometimes we need to limit our time with specific people or avoid certain places or activities. It's not easy. We need wisdom here, but God says He'll give us it to us—whenever we ask for it (James 1:5)!

5. Refresh your spirit. Specifically in song. There is something about the power of praise and worship to lift our hearts to God and draw his heart to ours. The Scripture tells us that God inhabits the praises of His people (Ps. 22:3 KJV). We experience

His presence in an incredible way when we worship Him. And when do we need His presence more than when we feel anxious, worried, or afraid?

When King Saul was tormented by an evil spirit, David would come and play his harp for him, play the psalms of praise and worship he had composed in the pasture as he watched over his sheep. The anger, fear, confusion, and paranoia that had filled Saul's heart began to dissipate. "Then relief would come to Saul; he would feel better, and the evil spirit would leave him" (1 Sam. 16:23).

I know when my own spirit is under attack, if I sing songs about the blood of Jesus that was shed for me and the victory that He won on Calvary—if I put praise and worship music on in the house or the car or my iPod, the atmosphere instantly changes. For me, it's a good thing—but for the enemy, it becomes extremely uncomfortable and unpleasant—and he leaves!

It's one reason Ephesians 5:19 urges us, "Speak to one another with psalms, hymns and spiritual songs. Sing and make music in your heart to the Lord." And Hebrews 13:15 describes a "sacrifice of praise" as a precious gift to be laid on the altar of God.

You may have to fight a battle more than once to win it.

—Margaret Thatcher

In my own spiritual journey, in my own battles with fear, these have definitely been the top five strategies for me. These are the ones that—when I've put them into practice—have been the most powerful, the most effective, the most life changing. But there are others that I use, too. Let me share five more with you:

1. Stay "purposefully" busy. I don't mean to suggest that any of us should add more pressure and stress to our already overcrowded schedules. I'm thinking of those times when we're waiting for something important . . . a phone call, an update, a decision, test results. Or when we find ourselves (for whatever reason) home alone—a lot. Times when we're particularly vulnerable to fear and worry if we don't have anything else to think about or anything else to do. The Scripture tells us to "be alert and on guard," knowing that our enemy loves to take advantage of these opportunities (1 Pet. 5:8). We're not unaware of his schemes (2 Cor. 2:11).

So we need to be proactive, purposefully busy. We've got to find something to occupy our minds and fill our time. Plan some activities, schedule get-togethers with friends, do puzzles, go to movies, get lost in good books. Take a class or take up a sport. Reorganize the closet. Fill out your younger children's baby books—even if they're in college now. Use this time to reach out to those in need (see the next strategy). Knit cozy blankets for chemotherapy patients or hats for the homeless. Volunteer at a soup kitchen or shelter; help build a house with Habitat for Humanity. Do something—don't just sit there and stew!

The best way to forget all your troubles is to wear tight shoes.

—Patsy Clairmont

2. Reach out. Particularly to those in need. Look for ways to encourage others. Fear has a way of making us very self-focused, even selfish and self-absorbed. It's important to remind ourselves constantly that we are not the only people in the world with problems. We are not the only people struggling or suffering. Galatians 6:10 says, "As we have opportunity, let us do good to all people." Write notes of encouragement, send e-mails, texts, or Facebook messages. Pick up the phone. Pray for others and their needs. Pray *with* them. Get involved in a cause or a missions outreach or a community service project. Sometimes it's easier to be brave for others. But the courage we summon for them has a way of spilling back into our own lives, too.

3. Get healthy. We all know that we feel better when we eat right, when we exercise, when we get fresh air and sunshine and a good night's rest. Our physical health really does affect our spiritual health and vice versa. I've learned the hard way that it's vitally important to take care of the body God has given me, so that I can have the energy and strength to do all that He's called me to do. I've seen for myself how exercise in particular seems to balance my emotional ups and downs, helps me to think more clearly and handle stressful situations better. I'm sorry, but it's true.* I've also learned that certain health issues and medications can either cause or contribute

---

*And no, it's not "easy for me to say." I've had eight major surgeries in the last five years. I was on bed rest and crutches for two of those years. I live with chronic pain. But I do what I can do. And so should you!

to feelings of anxiety, worry, or stress. So it's important to keep doctor's appointments and stay on top of those things, too.

4. Get help. Sometimes it can really help to see a counselor. It can help to talk to someone about all the anxious thoughts that have been swirling round and round in our heads, to say these things out loud to another human being who will listen and understand. A good counselor will be a sounding board—someone who will give us perspective, point us to the truth, and suggest some concrete steps we can take, things we can actually do. Some counselors specialize in helping people in crisis, offering support while we're working through a specific problem or dealing with a difficult situation. Others provide ongoing support for those who find it beneficial to talk to someone on a regular basis. For more information, see "When Should I Call a Counselor or Therapist?" on page 185.

5. Pair up with an Anatolian shepherd. Okay, this one takes a little more explaining, but bear with me. If you've ever been to a zoo or watched the Discovery Channel or Animal Planet, you probably know that cheetahs are the fastest animals in the world. They have great big claws that they use to push off with when they start running. They have really sharp teeth. To us, they look pretty fierce. But apparently they're great big scaredy-cats. So scared, so skittish that they're in danger of becoming extinct. They just don't socialize well. They're too nervous. Too anxious. Too stressed. Unless they have shepherds, that is. Anatolian shepherds.

It's a long story, and no one is exactly sure how a phenomenon first observed in the wild got reimagined and applied to cheetahs living in captivity. But somehow someone discovered that these dogs—these Anatolian shepherds—make great companions for scaredy-cats. For thousands of years, bold and courageous Anatolian shepherds have guarded sheep in Asia—fearlessly chasing off lions and tigers and bears . . . and cheetahs. Which has kept cheetahs alive, since sheep herders haven't felt the need to kill them to protect their flocks.

About forty years ago, wildlife conservationists discovered that when these brave dogs are paired with cheetahs in zoos and animal parks, they function as guardians for the cats. The dogs are patient and kind. They have a calming influence. Their presence makes the cheetahs feel safe and secure. And they relax. Over time, zookeepers have noticed that the dogs seem to model healthy behaviors like friendliness and playfulness and that the cheetahs learn these important life skills from them. (I'm not making this up.) And happy, relaxed cheetahs are more likely to be friendly with other happy, relaxed cheetahs, which leads to the pitter-patter of little happy, relaxed cheetah feet—which for wildlife conservationists is the point.[1]

To help us grow from scaredy-cats into lionhearts, we need to pair ourselves up with some shepherds. We all have the Chief Shepherd, of course. But He's given us others—brothers and sisters in Christ who are bold and courageous. These people have a calming influence on us. They make us feel safe. At the same time, they model for us confidence and courage. They teach us how to be brave and take risks and (gasp) have a little fun ourselves!

I love how Pam Farrel says, "My closest friends come in two sizes: those more courageous than I am—from whom I hope to catch courage, and those less courageous than I am—who want to catch courage from me."[2]

That's the ideal.

Because we don't have to face our fear alone—and we don't get bonus points for trying to. If we're smart, we'll take all the help we can get. And give all the help we can give.

A friend is someone who knows the song
in your heart and can sing it back to you
when you have forgotten the words.

—Anonymous

Fear is a bully—a big bully. And surrendering to it doesn't make it go away. Surrendering empowers it. Emboldens it. Makes it stronger and stronger, until it becomes a stronghold—a fortress the enemy has built in the battlefield of our minds.

The good news is that we don't have to surrender. We can resist. We can fight back. And we can win (Ps. 60:12)! We can even tear down strongholds (2 Cor. 10:4).

How is this possible?

> It is God who arms me with strength
> and makes my way perfect.
> He makes my feet like the feet of a deer;
> he enables me to stand on the heights.

He trains my hands for battle;
  my arms can bend a bow of bronze."
  (Ps. 18:32–34)

Let Him be your strength and your shield today.

Bible Study

1. Read 2 Chronicles 20:1–30. The tiny kingdom of Judah was under attack.

a) Why were the people afraid (v. 2)?

b) What did they do (vv. 3–4)?

c) What did King Jehoshaphat pray (v. 12)?

d) How did God answer? What did He say (vv. 15, 17)?

e) Who led the armies of Judah to the battlefield (v. 21)?

f) What happened (vv. 22–25)?

g) What was the end result (vv. 29–30)?

2. Turn to Psalm 9:10. What declaration does the psalmist make?

3. As you reflect on the story in 2 Chronicles 20 and the battle strategies we've talked about in this chapter, what stands out to you? What can you do this week—today—to start putting some of these truths into practice, applying these strategies to the battles you face?

4. Choose one of the following verses (or one mentioned previously in the chapter) to memorize and meditate on this week:

Ephesians 4:22–24	1 Thessalonians 5:16–18
Romans 12:1–2	Hebrews 10:23
Colossians 3:16	2 Thessalonians 2:16–17

5. Take a few moments to record any further thoughts or reflections in your journal.

chapter seven

Forged in the Flames

Only through experience of trial and suffering can the soul be strengthened.

—Helen Keller

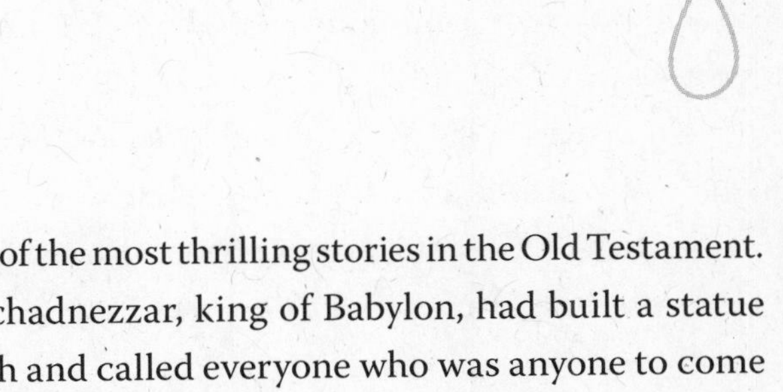

It's one of the most thrilling stories in the Old Testament. Nebuchadnezzar, king of Babylon, had built a statue ninety feet high and called everyone who was anyone to come and see it, come and witness the dedication ceremony. Come and worship the graven image. Publicly pledge your total allegiance, your unquestioning obedience, your faithful service to the king—or be thrown into a blazing furnace.

But Shadrach, Meshach, and Abednego could do no such thing. The band played and the rest of the crowd bowed, but the three men stood tall. Furious as he was, the king did not want to kill them. They were very valuable to him, his wisest advisors. He tried to give them another chance.

But Shadrach, Meshach, and Abednego made it clear that once again they would refuse to obey the king's decree. "If we are thrown into the blazing furnace, the God we serve is able to save us from it, and he will rescue us from your hand" (Dan. 3:17).

You can't help but be in awe of their courage. First of all, the courage it took to stand. And stay standing. The courage not only to trust God in their hearts and believe that He was able to save them but to declare that publicly before this pagan king and all these witnesses. Talk about putting yourself out there!

Yet their most courageous stand was still to come:

"But even if he does not, we want you to know, O king, that we will not serve your gods or worship the image of gold you have set up" (Dan. 3:18).

No matter what. We will still love God. We will still trust God. We will still serve God. Even if He does not do a miracle on our behalf. Even if He does not come to our rescue. Even if He does not spare us from a fiery death.

Even if He does not.

Courage is almost a contradiction in terms. It means a strong desire to live taking the form of a readiness to die.

—Gilbert K. Chesterton

Because sometimes He doesn't. And that's a fact. It's a reality we have to be prepared for. It's a very real part of facing our fear—knowing that God doesn't always intervene. Sometimes He does allow awful things to happen to us or to people we care about. Sometimes our fears come true, the things we dread do happen. We hope they won't. We know that most of the time, they don't. But we have to decide whether we'll trust God even when they do.

Because sometimes it is cancer. Sometimes it is a brain tumor. Sometimes it is diabetes or heart disease or blindness or . . .

Sometimes it is unemployment. Sometimes it is hunger or homelessness. Sometimes it is bankruptcy or financial ruin or . . .

Sometimes it is singleness. Sometimes it is divorce or widowhood. Sometimes it is childlessness or infertility. Sometimes it is having a prodigal or a parent who couldn't care less. Or . . .

Sometimes it is rejection. Sometimes it is betrayal. Sometimes it is persecution. Sometimes it is abuse or abandonment or neglect. Sometimes it is rape or domestic violence. Or . . .

Sometimes it is death. All kinds of death.

In Hebrews 11:33–35, we read about the triumphs of many of the great men and women of the Bible "who through faith conquered kingdoms, administered justice, and gained what was promised; who shut the mouths of lions, quenched the fury of the flames, and escaped the edge of the sword; whose weakness was turned to strength; and who became powerful in battle and routed foreign armies. Women received back their dead, raised to life again."

But then it goes on to say, "Others were tortured and refused to be released, so that they might gain a better resurrection. Some faced jeers and flogging, while still others were chained and put in prison. They were stoned; they were sawed in two; they were put to death by the sword. They went about in sheepskins and goatskins, destitute, persecuted and mistreated. . . .

They wandered in deserts and mountains, and in caves and holes in the ground" (vv. 35–38).

Here's how God inspired the writer of Hebrews to describe His beloved people, His faithful servants: "the world was not worthy of them" (v. 38).

The world was not worthy of them. But still He let them suffer all those terrible things.

They knew full well He might. They understood that going in.

And so should we.

God's people have always faced trials and tribulations, heartache and hardship, suffering and persecution, for a number of reasons.

For one thing, we live in a fallen world, a broken, imperfect world, a world cursed by sin and death. It's been that way since the beginning—well, since Adam and Eve (Gen. 3:1–24). Yes, Jesus has redeemed us from the curse, He has set us free from the power of sin and death (Gal. 3:13, Heb. 2:14–15). But the world itself has not yet been made new (Rom. 8:21, 2 Pet. 3:13). We are not home yet.

For another thing, we have an enemy who is out to get us. Really, he's out to get God. Or he'd like to be. But he can't—he's not powerful enough to take on God Himself in all His glory. So he tries to hurt God—to wound His heart—by destroying the beauty of His creation and by turning His precious children against Him and against each other. Ever since the garden, Satan has been wreaking havoc, filling people's hearts and minds with evil, causing as much trauma and tragedy—as much death and destruction—as he possibly can. Because he knows his days are numbered (Rev. 12:12). And God has allowed it only because it ultimately serves His purposes. It tests us and reveals what's in our hearts. It gives us a legitimate choice as to who or what we will trust, who or what we will serve. When we respond to suffering by putting a greater faith and trust in God, it draws us into an even deeper, more intimate relationship with Him (1 Pet. 1:6–7).

Then there's the world itself, meaning people who choose to be enemies of God, people who love darkness rather than light (John 3:19). Sometimes they're out to get us, too.

Jesus warned us about this a number of times. He told us not to be surprised: "If the world hates you, keep in mind that it hated me first. If you belonged to the world, it would love you as its own. As it is, you do not belong to the world, but I have chosen you out of the world. That is why the world hates you. . . . If they persecuted me, they will persecute you also" (John 15:18–20).

In Matthew 5:11–12, He added, "Blessed are you when people insult you, persecute you and falsely say all kinds of evil against you because of me. Rejoice and be glad, because great is your reward in heaven."

Then in John 16:33, He explained, "I have told you these things, so that in me you may have peace. In this world you will have trouble. But take heart! I have overcome the world."

> *[Real courage is] when you know you're licked*
> *before you begin but you begin anyway*
> *and you see it through no matter what.*
> —Harper Lee

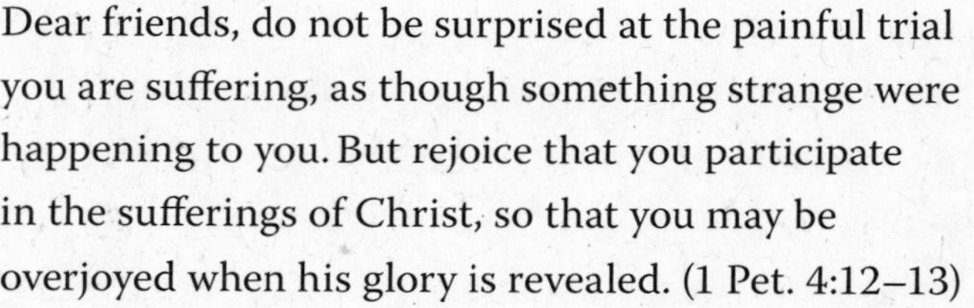

> Dear friends, do not be surprised at the painful trial you are suffering, as though something strange were happening to you. But rejoice that you participate in the sufferings of Christ, so that you may be overjoyed when his glory is revealed. (1 Pet. 4:12–13)

So much of the New Testament was written to believers who were facing the fear of hardship, suffering, and persecution. Most of the New Testament was written by believers who had already been through or were currently experiencing hardship, suffering, and persecution. If pain and suffering is practically promised to us, how can we NOT be afraid?

When the enemy tries to fill our heads with visions of all the horrible things that could be in store for us, all the things that could go terribly, terribly wrong, we know now that we can't comfort ourselves by saying, "God would never let that happen to me."

He might not. Then again, He might.

So what *can* we say?

In those desperate moments, when we feel the fear and panic rising, instead of trying to come up with a reassuring affirmation, I think we should consider asking ourselves a question. Or rather, three questions:

1. Not "Why me?" but "Why not me?" Why shouldn't I suffer (whatever it is)? Why shouldn't I have to experience this? Other people do. Millions of people on this planet have faced the same kinds of hardships, the same trials, the same sufferings. Many of them have experienced far worse. I don't have to look very far to see someone I wouldn't want to trade places with. Someone whose trials seem impossibly overwhelming to me. And there are people who feel the same way about me! I know it's a privilege to share in the fellowship of Christ's sufferings (Phil. 3:7–11).

But if I do look far . . . back in time, to a Nazi death camp, for instance. Or across the ocean to a place where starving children dig through garbage heaps to find food to eat. Down a dark alley where other women are being trafficked and enslaved. Or to a country where my brothers and sisters in Christ are even now—this very hour—being tortured and executed for their faith . . .

I have nothing to say.

I can only fall on my face before God and thank Him for the sufferings He has specially chosen—handpicked—for me. That He knows best the cross that I can bear. And pray that if the day comes that He asks me to bear one of these other things that haunt me, one of these things I fear or dread, that in that moment I'll have the courage and strength to pass the test. To bear it well and bring glory and honor to His name.

> And the God of all grace, who called you to his eternal glory in Christ, after you have suffered a little while, will himself restore you and make you strong, firm and steadfast. To him be the power for ever and ever. Amen. (1 Pet. 5:10–11)

I had feelings of fear about the future. . . . The devil kept on whispering, "It's all right now, but what about afterward? You are going to be very lonely." . . . And I turned to my God in a kind of desperation and said, "Lord, what can I do? How can I go on to the end?" And He said, "None of them that trust in Me shall be desolate." That word has been with me ever since.

—Amy Carmichael

---

2. Where else can we go? During his earthly ministry, Jesus said a lot of things that people didn't understand. He said a lot of things that people didn't want to hear. Sometimes truth is like that. Hard to hear. Hard to understand.

John 6:60–69 tells us that after one sermon, it wasn't just the Pharisees who were offended. Even Jesus' followers exclaimed, "This is a hard teaching. Who can accept it?"

From this time, the Scripture says, many of His disciples turned back and no longer followed Him. Then Jesus looked to the Twelve and asked them a piercing question:

> "You do not want to leave too, do you?"

Simon Peter responded simply: "Lord, to whom shall we go? You have the words of eternal life. We believe and know that you are the Holy One of God."

And that's really what it all comes down to, isn't it?

We don't always understand God. We don't always like what He chooses to do, what He allows in our lives, what He asks us to do. What He asks us to endure. There are times when we're hurt and angry, times we're afraid. Times when our faith is almost shattered.

But where else can we go? Who else can we go to? There is nowhere else. There is no one else. Only Jesus has the words of eternal life—we know that He is the Son of God. So we hold on to Him as tight as we can, and we learn to say with Job (a man who knew a thing or two about suffering): "Though he slay me, yet will I hope in him" (Job 13:15).

3. What's the worst that can happen? A few years ago, author Joshua Piven created a series of best-selling books beginning with the *Worst Case Scenario Survival Handbook*—in which he provided real, accurate, step-by-step instructions for readers who were afraid they might one day need to know how to escape from quicksand, survive an earthquake, kick down a door, jump from a moving car, wrestle an alligator, land a plane, defuse a bomb, or deliver a baby in a taxicab. It's genius, isn't it? Be prepared for everything—and I mean everything—that could possibly go wrong, no matter how unlikely, and you have nothing to fear.

Of course, it's not really possible to prepare yourself for every worst case scenario. But asking the question—"What's the worst that can happen?"—is a good place to start. In fact, I'd go so far as to say it may very well be one of the most important questions that, as believers, we can teach our anxious minds and fearful hearts to raise.

I'll show you what I mean. Take any situation, any scenario, that is causing you fear or dread and ask yourself: "What's the worst that can happen?" When you've answered the question, ask another: "Okay, and then what?" And after that, "Then what?" Take it as far down that dark, miserable road as you can. It's where your mind keeps trying to make you go anyway. This time, go ahead—all the way.

I'll give you a hint: no matter what crisis or trial or worst case scenario you start with and how many steps it takes you to get there, the second-to-last answer is always "and then I (or we) die a miserably slow and painful, agonizing death." Worst case, remember? Which, no matter how slow, can only last so long. (Think how fast the last year has gone by!)

And then what?

And then we're safe in the arms of Jesus. At home in heaven, forever. In a place where evil can never reach us, never threaten us or harm us again. A place where there's no hurt, no heartache, no suffering or pain.

Think about it. For those of us who love Him, every possible scenario ends the same way. When we look at it like that, it changes everything.

You know, in the days after Jesus' death and resurrection, the good news of the Gospel was spreading like wildfire. The early church grew at an alarming rate—at least it was alarming to their enemies. That was the first time the church began to suffer state-sponsored persecution. Many of Jesus' disciples were imprisoned, tortured, and executed for their faith.

At one point, King Herod had arrested Simon Peter, planning to bring him to trial after Passover. Herod had him guarded by a squad of sixteen men. Peter was chained between two of the soldiers around the clock. But, in spite of Herod's schemes, it wasn't Peter's time to go. God still had work for him to do. The night before the trial, an angel of the Lord appeared and a light shone in the cell. He struck Peter on the side and woke him up. "'Get up, Peter,'" he said, and the chains fell off Peter's wrists (Acts 12:7).

Anything about that scenario strike you as a bit odd—besides the angelic visitation, I mean? Think about it . . . if you were in a prison cell, knowing you would be executed in the morning, what would you be doing? Anxiously pacing the floor? Wringing your hands? Crying out to God in fear and desperation? Or sleeping so soundly someone would have to hit you to wake you up?

How did he do it? How could Peter sleep at a time like this? In a word, trust. Peter trusted God utterly and completely. He knew his life was in the hands of his Heavenly Father. One way or another, it would turn out all right. If he lived, God would be with him. If he died, he'd be with God. Either way, it was okay with him.

Paul talked about the same thing when he said that "to be absent from the body" was to be "present with the Lord" (2 Cor. 5:8). He told the church in Philippi that, honestly, he felt a little conflicted when he looked at all the times his life had been in jeopardy: "I desire to depart and be with Christ, which is better by far; but it is more necessary for you that I remain in the body" (Phil. 1:23–24).

Remember in Hebrews 11:35 where it said that some "refused to be released, so that they might gain a better resurrection"? They understood that being rescued or raised from the dead is wonderful, if God has a purpose in it—if He still has work for you to do. But everyone that was ever raised from the dead in Scripture died again later. Peter, who was rescued by an angel one time, was crucified another.

In this world, pain and suffering and death cannot be avoided. But the good news is that this world is not "as good as it gets." At least, not for us.

Author Randy Alcorn makes a powerful observation: for unbelievers, actually, it is.[1] For those who choose not to trust in Jesus—those who refuse His salvation—this world is as close to heaven as they will ever get. This world full of war, poverty, famine, disease, hardship and heartache, betrayal, and disappointment is as much paradise as they will ever experience. It only goes downhill from here. All the way down into hell, eternal separation from God. Far away and far apart from anything that is good or true or kind or loving, anything pleasant or happy or beautiful. Anything creative or inspiring and uplifting.

But, for those of us who do choose Jesus, those who do believe in Him and trust Him and love Him and serve Him, this world is as close to hell as we will ever get. This is the most hardship, the most difficulty, the most pain, the most evil we will ever face. And it's over before we know it, gone in a flash. From here, it only gets better and better. And better.

So how can we be afraid?

Martin Luther had it right. Luther was a man who was passionate about his faith in Christ, committed to exposing corruption in the church and holding it to the highest standards, insisting on making the Word of God available to ordinary people in a language they could understand. It cost him dearly—Luther was outlawed, exiled, threatened with torture and death. But, through it all, he learned that the devil had nothing on him; neither his human enemies nor the enemy of his soul was any match for the power of God. Nearly five hundred years ago, Luther penned these words:

> A mighty fortress is our God,
> a bulwark never failing;
> Our helper He, amid the flood
> of mortal ills prevailing:
> For still our ancient foe
> doth seek to work us woe;
> His craft and pow'r are great,
> and armed with cruel hate,
> on earth is not his equal.
>
> Did we in our own strength confide,
> our striving would be losing;
> Were not the right Man on our side,

the Man of God's own choosing:
Dost ask who that may be?
Christ Jesus, it is He;
Lord of Hosts, His Name,
from age to age the same,
And He must win the battle.

And though this world, with devils filled,
should threaten to undo us,
we will not fear, for God hath willed
His truth to triumph through us;
The Prince of Darkness grim,
we tremble not for him;
His rage we can endure,
for lo! his doom is sure,
One little word shall fell him.

That word above all earthly pow'rs,
no thanks to them, abideth;
The Spirit and the gifts are ours
through Him Who with us sideth:
Let goods and kindred go,
this mortal life also;
The body they may kill:
God's truth abideth still,
His kingdom is forever.
Hallelujah!
(A Mighty Fortress Is Our God)

In 2 Corinthians 4:16–18, Paul exclaimed, "Therefore we do not lose heart. Though outwardly we are wasting away, yet inwardly we are being renewed day by day. For our light and momentary troubles are achieving for us an eternal glory that far outweighs them all. So we fix our eyes not on what is seen, but on what is unseen. For what is seen is temporary, but what is unseen is eternal."

Ultimately that's how we face fear—with our eyes firmly fixed on our eternal hope and our glorious Savior.

The most important part of our task will be to tell everyone who will listen that Jesus is the only answer to the problems that are disturbing the hearts of men and nations. We shall have the right to speak because we can tell from our experience that His light is more powerful than the deepest darkness. . . . How wonderful that the reality of His presence is greater than the reality of the hell around us.

—Betsie Ten Boom, speaking to her sister Corrie, while they were imprisoned in a Nazi concentration camp

---

Bible Study

1. Spend a few minutes reading the first two chapters of the book of Job. What do we know—that Job didn't know—about his suffering? (1:6–12; 2:1–6) What purpose did it serve?

2. Even though he didn't see the big picture, he didn't know the whole story—even though he couldn't have understood what was happening to him or why—how did Job respond? (1:20–22; 2:10)

3. If you continue reading through the book of Job, you'll find he did ask some honest questions. He debated the nature of suffering and the nature of God himself with those who came to "comfort" (or really, to accuse) him. Eventually, God answered Job, though not the way he expected. Read Job 42. How does the story end?

4. Turn to Psalm 40. The psalmist rejoiced that God had at last delivered him from his suffering. According to Psalm 40:3, what did God give him? What greater purpose did this serve?

5. Can you think of an example from your own life—a greater purpose that some of your sufferings have already served?

6. Choose one of the following verses (or one mentioned previously in the chapter) to memorize or meditate on this week:

Psalm 27:1	Isaiah 35:3–4
Psalm 119:114	James 1:12
John 14:27	Romans 16:20

7. Take a few moments to record any further thoughts or reflections.

chapter eight

Fearless!

Don't wish me happiness—I don't expect to be happy. It's gotten beyond that, somehow. Wish me courage and strength and a sense of humor—I will need them all.

—Anne Morrow Lindbergh

The Apostle Peter was writing a letter to some very courageous Christians going through tough times. He paused in the middle of his letter to include a special note to some particularly courageous women—women who believed in Jesus and put their faith in Him, even when their husbands did not (1 Pet. 3:1–6). Remember that this was at a time when, culturally, most women were routinely denied what we could consider basic human rights, including the right to an education, the right to an occupation, property ownership, religious and political freedom. Choosing to become a follower of Jesus Christ—without her husband's approval or consent—was a pretty bold move for any woman.

But these women had experienced the life-changing power of the gospel. They knew the love of Christ. They knew the forgiveness of their sins. They knew the new life God had already given them and the eternal life He had promised them. Naturally they were eager for their husbands to share the experience. They wanted their husbands to come to know Jesus, too. And they may have been tempted (as women in the same position have been, ever since) to try to make it happen. Trying in their own wisdom, in their own strength, going about it in all the wrong ways. But Peter gave these women some wise advice—advice that we can apply to so many different areas of our lives today.

He explained that it wouldn't do any good to preach all the time—or nag, or whine, or argue. You can't harangue or harass anyone into trusting in Christ. Manipulation and seduction—not effective here, either. Peter said that, instead, these women should live out their faith on a daily basis and set a good example. They should treat their husbands with sincere and genuine respect, something that all men seem to be hardwired to crave—even above love and affection. Let them take the lead, as God has called them to. Be encouraging and supportive of their efforts to protect and provide for the family. This kind of loving attitude is a far more effective way to show an unbelieving husband the difference that faith in Jesus makes. (As it happens, this is exactly how my grandmother led my grandfather to trust in Christ. Years later he would say, "I just couldn't believe that she fell in love with another Man . . . but I also couldn't deny that loving Him somehow made her love me more!")

As he explained all of this in his letter, Peter made a couple of fascinating observations about fear. And that's really what I want to focus on. He pointed to Sarah as an example of a woman who was respectful of her husband and his leadership—and then added: "You are her daughters if you do what is right and do not give way to fear" (1 Pet. 3:6).

It seems that Sarah's most outstanding virtue or character quality—the one that we are to emulate—is that she was not fearful or anxious. She did not give way to fear. So what does this have to do with her "obedience" to Abraham? Well, when you read Sarah's story in Genesis 12–23, you know she didn't choose to "obey" him or "submit" to him out of fear. Not hardly. She let Abraham lead their family, but she could take control whenever she wanted to. We know this because of the times she did—with spectacularly disastrous results. No, Sarah wasn't afraid of Abraham. I think that's one of the points Peter is making. We don't respect and obey those in authority over us out of fear of them. We don't live in cowering fear of other human beings or allow that fear to dominate, control, or destroy us. We fear God. And because we fear (respect) Him, we respect other authorities He has established or put into place.*

Back to Sarah. She also didn't follow Abraham's lead because she trusted him so completely—because she thought he was infallible. She knew better than that. At times Abraham showed some spectacularly poor judgment of his own. So how could Sarah trust Abraham and follow (submit to) his leadership?

---

* It's important to note that this passage of Scripture does not counsel women to submit to evil—to force themselves to participate in sinful behavior at the behest of their husbands or to silently suffer violence or abuse. Such an interpretation clearly disregards the whole counsel of God—the numerous Scriptures that teach otherwise. "The prudent see danger and take refuge" (Prov. 27:12). If you are in danger, be courageous enough to get help—and get out of harm's way immediately. For more on the Biblical response to abusive relationships, see Leslie Vernick's books listed in the Recommended Resources.

The short answer is, she didn't. She didn't trust Abraham. She trusted God. And that's why she wasn't afraid to follow Abraham. She knew that God was leading Abraham and that if Abraham disobeyed God, if Abraham missed God, if Abraham got off course—then God would deal with Abraham, one way or another (Prov. 3:25). Which He did. Repeatedly.

Sarah's trust was in God. That's why she wasn't afraid to pack up everything, leave her country, her people, her family, and traipse off to who knows where, following Abraham, who was following God—"to a land that I will show you" (Gen. 12:1). It's why she wasn't afraid to begin the many adventures that took them through Egypt and Canaan, led to the birth of their son Isaac, and made them the father and mother of many nations, of kings, of peoples, with descendants as numerous as the stars in the sky and the sand on the seashore.

Even when Sarah ran out ahead of God and tried to make things happen, it wasn't because she didn't believe in God's plan or purpose for them. She just thought He needed a little help getting it done. (What woman hasn't thought that, at one time or another?)

Scripture tells us that Sarah was a beautiful woman. She was so beautiful that when she was in her sixties or seventies, she was desired by Pharaoh, the king of Egypt, who tried to take her into his harem.

Peter tells us what really made Sarah beautiful—what makes any woman beautiful—is not her outward beauty, not her jewelry or makeup or fashion sense, but her "inner self, the unfading beauty of a gentle and quiet spirit, which is of great worth in God's sight" (1 Pet. 3:4). Some translations say "a peaceful spirit," "calm" or "tranquil" or "gracious." The Amplified Bible adds "not anxious or wrought up."

Not restless, not irritable or uptight, not worried, not stressed out, not obsessive, not striving, not deeply insecure, not neurotic, not despondent, not . . . fearful.

It comes back to fear. What makes us beautiful to God and to others is that inner beauty that comes from peace, from faith, from trust. Confidence—not in ourselves, but in our God and who we are in Him. Courage.

Living fearlessly. That's what makes us beautiful. That's what makes us free. That's what makes us the women God meant for us to be.

I believe in being strong when everything seems to be going wrong. I believe that happy girls are the prettiest girls. I believe that tomorrow is another day, and I believe in miracles.

—Audrey Hepburn

But what does it mean to be fearless? To live fearlessly? I think first we have to know what living fearlessly does not mean:

Living fearlessly does not mean you never make any noise! You can have a "gentle and quiet spirit," a deep sense of peace, an inner calm, a steady strength and resolve—while you reach for your helmet, strap on your sword, and get ready to ride out into battle! During his earthly ministry, Jesus made a lot of noise. He confronted sin, exposed wickedness and corruption, stood up for the poor and the oppressed. He reached out to those who were lost, those who were hurting. And not just when they reached out to Him. He went looking for them. He met them where they were. His behavior was considered scandalous by the society of the day. Ours may be, as well. Maybe you've heard the expression "Well-behaved women rarely make history!" If "well-behaved" means living by society's standards, living for the world's approval and applause, then God has not called us to be well-behaved. He hasn't called us to be nice and quiet and never make any waves. He's called us to be good. He's called us to be righteous and holy and radically obedient to Him. He's called us to live our faith out loud!

Living fearlessly does not mean you never feel afraid. Sometimes you do still feel fear—but you don't let it consume you or control you. You let it serve you. Let it alert you, either to a real danger you need to guard against or a heart condition you need to address. And you remember that courage is not the absence of fear; it's the determination that something else is more important. It's the willingness to act in spite of it. The triumph over it.

Living fearlessly does not mean you never fall or fail. Being human, you will fall and fail all the time. No matter how much you resolve to never be afraid again, to be completely courageous from here on out. . . . Remember how Peter proudly proclaimed that he would never turn his back on Jesus, he would follow him to the death, right before (out of fear) he denied even knowing Jesus—three times? (Luke 22:31–34,

54–60). You're going make mistakes. And you're going to learn from them. You're going to struggle, you're going to stumble. You're going to fall on the mercy of God and extend that same mercy to others.

Living fearlessly does not mean living by someone else's definition of courage or bravery. It does not mean trying to force yourself to meet other people's standards or expectations. Or measuring your own courage or bravery by comparing yours to theirs. You are not them. They are not you. God's call on their lives is not His call on yours. What He is asking of them is not what He is asking of you. What represents a huge leap of faith—a real test of courage—for one person may be totally different for another. Don't let anyone, including yourself, belittle those steps of faith or rob you of the thrill of what God has been doing in you and through you, all the battles being fought and won. Do be open to being challenged to take even bigger steps—by the Holy Spirit and by trusted friends who know you well and have your best interests at heart. Be encouraged and inspired by those who are further along in the journey, those who've reached a place where you'd one day like to be. But if you find yourself trying to prove your bravery and courage by doing things that others decree to earn their approval or respect—that's succumbing to peer pressure. Out of fear. Courage is not caring what others think . . . about how courageous you are.

Now let's talk about what living fearlessly does mean. Living fearlessly means being **BOLD:**

B—Believing God. Believing He is who He says He is and that He will do all He says He will do. Trusting Him. Putting your faith in Him completely. In the words of Jesus, "Do not fear, only believe" (Luke 8:50 ESV).

O—Obeying God. "Faith in its active form is obedience."[1] Obeying God's Word, all of it, including the parts that say not to fear, not to worry, not to be anxious! Obeying Him in all the other areas of our lives, too. Obeying Him when He calls us to be bold and courageous and step out in faith. "Do not merely listen to the word. . . . Do what it says" (James 1:22).

L—Living Fully. Being present. Experiencing the beauty and the blessing of this life, with all its joys and sorrows. Embracing the adventure. "All the days of the desponding *and* afflicted are made evil [by anxious thoughts and forebodings], but he who has a glad heart has a continual feast [regardless of circumstances]" (Prov. 15:15 AMP).

D—Daring to Dream. To imagine, to envision what God has called you to, why He has given you all the gifts and talents and insights and experience He's given you. How He might want to use those gifts for His kingdom and His glory. He is "able, through his mighty power at work within us, to accomplish infinitely more than we might ask or think" (Eph. 3:20 NLT). The NIV says "immeasurably more" than we can "imagine." So dream for yourself, for your

> family, for your community, for a lost and dying world in desperate need.

For you, living fearlessly may also mean learning to become more authentic, more real, more open and honest. Or it may mean learning to be more guarded, more wise and discerning. It may mean learning to be open to new things, to say, "Yes—why not?" instead of automatically saying, "No way!" Then again, it may mean learning to set boundaries, to say no to obligations and commitments you feel pressured to accept.

It's something to think about, something to pray about. Something to talk over with your friends and family. Ask Jesus to show you what He wants living fearlessly to look like for you!

I am not funny. My writers were funny.
My direction was funny. The situations were funny.
But I am not funny. What I am is brave.

—Lucille Ball

There are dozens and dozens of courageous women in Scripture—women who learned to live fearlessly. But it looked different for each one of them. Some of them risked life and limb; others risked ridicule or rejection, scandal or a ruined reputation. Some women stepped outside their comfort zone, left behind the familiar, and learned to lead a new and different life. Some stepped up in a desperate time and did what had to be done, when no one else could or would do it. Some spoke up for truth and justice. Some spoke up on behalf of themselves, their children, or their families. Let's look at just a few of them:

Shiphrah and Puah: These two Hebrew midwives defied a direct order from Pharaoh and refused to kill all the baby boys they delivered. Instead, they shielded them and protected them, saving hundreds of young lives (Exod. 1:17).

Jochebed: The mother of one of these baby boys had the courage to save her son by letting him go. She hid Moses in a basket and set him afloat on the river, because she knew that God had a call on his life and trusted that He would take care of him (Exod. 2:1–10, Heb. 11:23).

Miriam: The young girl faithfully kept watch over the baby, and then bravely spoke up when Pharaoh's daughter drew him out of the water, cleverly suggesting her own mother—the baby's mother—to be his nurse (Exod. 2:1–10).

Mahlah, Noah, Hoglah, Milcah, and Tirzah: The daughters of Zelophehad had no brothers. When their father died, they knew if they did not take action, his name would be forgotten and their family inheritance lost. They pleaded their case before Moses and a law was put in place to provide for daughters to inherit, as well as sons (Num. 27:1–11).

Deborah: This judge and ruler of Israel, the original warrior princess, led the armies of Israel into battle when they refused to go without her. Speaking prophetically, she warned them that a woman would get the glory for their victory (Judg. 4–5).

Jael: The woman Deborah spoke of, this wife and mother warmly welcomed the enemy general when he fled the battlefield.

She kindly let him rest in her tent, and, while he was sleeping, sweetly put a tent peg through his head (Judg. 4:17–21).

Ruth: The young widow left everything about her old life behind to become a loyal and faithful companion to her widowed mother-in-law, adopting Naomi's country, her culture, her faith, and her God as her own. Ruth bravely opened her heart to a new life and a new love (Ruth 1:16).

Abigail: The discerning woman who recognized her foolish husband's mistake in insulting the future king of Israel. She took action immediately, saving her whole household, by riding out to meet David with generous gifts—not the least of which were her wise counsel and words of encouragement (1 Sam. 25).

The Widow at Zarephath: Though she and her young son were literally starving to death, she obeyed God and gave their very last meal to the prophet Elijah, only to find that, from then on, her cupboard was never empty (1 Kings 17:7–16).

The Servant Girl: Taken captive, stolen from her homeland, and forced to work as a slave, the little girl didn't have to care about her master's health problems. She might even have gotten in trouble for speaking up. But that didn't stop her from telling Naaman about the prophet Elisha and the one true God who could heal him of his leprosy (2 Kings 5:3).

Jehosheba: This daughter of a king and wife of a priest ran to the royal nursery, snatched up the crown prince—her nephew—and hid him, right before all of the other young princes were murdered. She kept Joash alive and in hiding until his villainous grandmother could be dethroned and his kingdom returned to him (2 Chron. 22:11).

Courage is found in unlikely places.

—J. R. R. Tolkien

Esther: The young orphan turned beauty queen risked her husband's wrath and the threat of certain death to save her people—the entire Jewish nation—from utter and complete annihilation (Esther 1–10).

Elizabeth: She believed God and bore a son she named John—even when the rest of the family protested—because that's what God said to call him. Then she uttered the first prophetic words spoken by a human being in the New Testament era, prophesying over Mary, her kinswoman, boldly declaring the child in Mary's womb to be the Messiah (Luke 1:46).

Mary: This young woman surrendered all of her own plans, all of her own hopes and dreams, to become the mother of Jesus. Her life would be completely turned upside down. Her reputation would be ruined. She would be the subject of gossip and rumors for years to come. And, when her Son began His ministry . . . when He began to suffer, she would suffer in ways she couldn't begin to imagine. Yet she yielded herself so humbly, so willingly, so fully, so completely to the will of God (Luke 1:38).

The many women named and unnamed: They were among Jesus' first disciples, they traveled everywhere with Him as part of a larger group of His followers; the Scriptures say they helped support Him and His ministry out of their own income (Luke 8:1–3).

The Woman with the Issue of Blood: She courageously believed that though many doctors had failed her, Jesus could help her. She expressed her faith that He was the Messiah by reaching out for the hem of His garment—and received His healing power (Mark 5:24–34).

The Sinful Woman Who Anointed Jesus' Feet: She risked scorn and ridicule and rejection by daring to enter the house of a Pharisee to express her love for Jesus, pouring out a costly perfume to anoint Him, washing His feet with her tears (Luke 7:36–50).

The Syrophoenician (Greek) Woman: Her daughter was demon possessed. This desperate mother entered a Jewish home and approached a Jewish rabbi, determined to get help from the only One she knew who could give it. Jesus tested her with a question that might have made others wilt, but her brave answer revealed not only her determination but her depth. It won His praise and her daughter's healing (Mark 7:24–30).

The women at the foot of the cross: They didn't run away. They didn't hide. They stayed with Jesus through his agony on the cross, hour after hour, suffering with Him, then witnessing His resurrection (Matt. 27:55; Mark 15:41; Luke 23:49).

The women mentioned throughout the New Testament: These women opened their homes and their hearts to the gospel; they were actively involved in ministry, risking everything, giving everything to impact lives for the kingdom of God.

They were women of all different races, different nationalities. Women in different ages and stages of life. Some were married, some single; some young, some old; some rich, some poor. None of them were perfect. They all made mistakes. They had their moments. But "their weakness was turned to strength" (Heb. 11:34). And through them God's glory was revealed.

I alone cannot change the world, but I can cast a stone across the waters to create many ripples.

—Mother Teresa

And what about all the courageous women in history? The fearless women who have made a difference in our world today? Thousands and thousands of them. Names we would all know. And names none of us know. Women who chose to face their fear and conquer it or rise above it. Women God used in amazing ways to do amazing things for Him.

You can join them. You can be one of those women, if you want to. If you're willing—or willing to be made willing.

I say this with every confidence, because ultimately it's not about you and your bravery or you and your ability, you and your power or your strength or your determination or your anything. . . . It's about the Spirit of God working in and through you.

> Remember, dear brothers and sisters, that few of you were wise in the world's eyes or powerful or wealthy when God called you. Instead, God chose things the world considers foolish in order to shame those who think they are wise. And he chose things that are

> powerless to shame those who are powerful. God chose things despised by the world, things counted as nothing at all, and used them to bring to nothing what the world considers important. (1 Cor. 1:26–28 NLT)

Second Corinthians 4:7 explains, "We now have this light shining in our hearts, but we ourselves are like fragile clay jars containing this great treasure. This makes it clear that our great power is from God, not from ourselves" (NLT).

Shortly after Jesus ascended into heaven, Peter and John were preaching in the city of Jerusalem. More than five thousand men came to faith in Christ as a result, not counting the women and children. The Pharisees and other religious leaders were upset, and they called the two men to appear before them for questioning. I love what it says in Acts 4:13:

> When they saw the courage of Peter and John and realized that they were unschooled, ordinary men, they were astonished and they took note that these men had been with Jesus.

Where do we find the strength—the courage—to live fearlessly? By being with Jesus. Spending as much time as we can in his presence. Sticking close to him.

And that's exactly what—if we let it—our fear can drive us to do. It can be such an incredible gift, an unspeakable blessing, when facing our fear forces us to fully rely on Him.

Bible Study

1. Look up 2 Corinthians 1:3–5. We've talked about how our fear can cause us to cry out to God and how facing our fear can help us learn and grow. According to this passage, what other benefits do our trials and tribulations bring?

2. Choose one of the brave women of the Bible listed in this chapter and look up her story. If you have time, use a concordance or the study tools on a site like www.BibleGateway.com to find any other references to her in Scripture, any additional information. How was this woman fearless? What do you find most intriguing about her? What can you learn from her?

3. Think of some women whose courage has inspired you—women in Scripture, women in history, or women you know.

Jot down a few names and why each one speaks to you or what you have learned from her.

4. Think of the women in your own sphere of influence, women who are watching you, maybe even looking up to you—women in your family, in your workplace, in your church and community. What kind of example are you setting for them? What are you teaching them? What could you be teaching them?

5. Read Psalm 139:1–18; 23–24. Underline key words and phrases. Make verses 23–24 your personal prayer, as you ask God to show you areas of your heart and life in which He wants you to grow.

6. Choose one of the following verses (or one mentioned previously in the chapter) to memorize or meditate on this week:

Joshua 1:9	Titus 2:11–14
Luke 21:19	Hebrews 12:1–2
2 Peter 1:5–8	Revelation 1:17–18

7. Take a few moments to record any further thoughts or reflections.

Afterword

I have a hat. It is graceful and feminine and gives me a certain dignity, as if I were attending a state funeral or something. Someday I may get up enough courage to wear it, instead of carrying it.

—Erma Bombeck

Someday . . .

It's a process, isn't it? Every one of us is on our own journey. And we walk at our own pace—because we're all at different ages and stages. We have our own unique personalities and temperaments, we come from different backgrounds, we had different upbringings, we have different life experiences. We all have our own challenges to face, our own obstacles to overcome. Our own opportunities to learn and grow.

James 1:2–4 tells us, "Consider it pure joy, my brothers, whenever you face trials of many kinds, because you know that the testing of your faith develops perseverance. Perseverance must finish its work so that you may be mature and complete, not lacking anything."

Facing fear is most definitely a trial, a test of our faith. For most of us, it's a constant—or at least ongoing—battle. It's not just won and done.

In my own life I've found myself comparing it to the carnival game Whac-A-Mole. Remember that one? You stand in front of a counter full of holes. Up pops a pesky critter and you whack him with a mallet. Then up pops another one in a different spot. You whack that one, and another one pops up. It happens over and over. No sooner do you smack one down, another one takes its place. That's the nature of the game.

It could get really discouraging. (Okay, sometimes it does.) Why can't we just beat this thing? Why can't we be done with it, once and for all? But there are a few things we need to keep in mind:

1. Ultimately and for all eternity, the game has already been won. Jesus accomplished that Himself on the cross. One day He will call you into His glorious presence, into your true home in heaven with Him—a place so beautiful that it defies description, so wonderful that it's beyond imagination, a place where there is no fear, no pain, no suffering. So, no matter how defeated you feel on any given day, victory is yours. You are already a winner. "The God of peace will soon crush Satan under your feet" (Rom. 16:20).

2. Until then, while you live and breathe on this earth, you are in the game—whether you like it or not. And, unlike the carnival game, in real life the "moles" you face don't stay in their little cabinet. If you don't beat them back, they jump out and aim for your jugular. So not fighting is not an option. You better keep your mallet handy.

3. The more you practice your skills, the faster you get. The stronger you get. The better you play. Eventually you get to a place where most days you don't even break a sweat. Whacking and smacking those pesky critters becomes second nature, an automatic reflex. They don't get very far with you anymore. And as an added bonus, all that mallet wielding gives your inner warrior princess the kind of spiritual muscle—the lean, sculpted arms—that would make any athlete or supermodel jealous.

4. When the game is over, you don't just get a measly pile of tickets to exchange for cheap junk at the prize counter—or a meaningless high score. You get rewards in heaven! The Bible doesn't explain exactly what these rewards are and it's hard for us to imagine them, but from what we know of the love of God, what we can see of His creativity and ingenuity and thoughtfulness and generosity toward us, they must be amazing. Jesus mentioned them repeatedly as something we should look forward to (See Matt. 16:27; Rev. 22:12). And while the "game" is still in progress, every battle you fight, every battle you win is an expression of your love for Him, your trust in Him, your obedience to Him. It's a twofer, really: you bring glory to God and give the devil a black eye at the same time. You also have the privilege of being an example, an inspiration, an encouragement—maybe even a mentor—to other players.

So don't give up. Don't give in. No matter how long it takes. Wherever you are on your journey, keep moving forward. Step by step, day by day. Keep learning, keep growing. Keep challenging yourself to step outside your comfort zone. Dare to do new and different things you've only dreamed of. Things you've never dreamed of! Be bold and courageous. Wear beautiful hats instead of carrying them—or looking longingly at them from outside the store window!

Of course there are days when beautiful hats are the furthest thing from your mind. Dark days, when your journey takes a turn you didn't expect. Days when the road seems long and the way uncertain. It takes all the courage you have just to put one foot in front of the other. You're not sure you can take another step.

Luke 24:13–35 tells us of a time when two of Jesus' disciples felt that way. They were terribly confused, deeply discouraged. Lonely and afraid. Their world had fallen to pieces. Everything they thought they knew. It seemed like God Himself had turned His back on them. Turned His back on Jesus. Left Him to die on the cross. As far as the disciples were concerned, the situation could not have been more desperate, more hopeless.

Weary and heavyhearted, they headed down the road to Emmaus. A Stranger came and walked along beside them. Before they knew it, they were pouring their hearts out to Him, telling Him all their troubles.

Then it was the Stranger's turn to speak. He took them back through the story they had just told Him and told it to them—from a completely different perspective. He filled in all kinds of details they had never noticed, told them all the things they hadn't seen and explained the meaning of the things they had. The Light was beginning to dawn on them.

As night drew near, they reached the village where the disciples intended to stay, and it seemed the Stranger was about to leave them. They begged Him not to go but stay and join them for the evening meal. As He gave thanks and broke the bread, their eyes were opened. Finally, they could see. It was Jesus himself. He had been with them all the time.

The disciples' experience on the road to Emmaus speaks so powerfully to us today. It reminds us that, in our darkest moments, help will come. Jesus will come. He will walk beside us. He will comfort us with His presence. He will open our eyes to His truth and show us things we've never seen before. He will bring us out of darkness into His wonderful light.

What a precious promise! What a glorious hope!

> Therefore we will not fear. (Ps. 46:2)

In the words of St. Augustine:

God of our life,

There are days when the burdens we carry chafe our shoulders and weigh us down; when the road seems dreary and endless, the skies gray and threatening; when our lives have no music in them, and our hearts are lonely, and our souls have lost their courage.

Flood the path with light, we beseech Thee; turn our eyes to where the skies are full of promise; tune our hearts to brave music; give us the sense of comradeship with heroes and saints of every age; and so quicken our spirits that we may be able to encourage the souls of all who journey with us on the road of life, to Thy honor and glory.

Amen

Questions Women Ask

When Should I Call a Counselor or Therapist?

Sometimes we need help to face our fears—more help than our friends and family are willing or able to give. Sometimes the issues are more complicated than even we realize! It can help to talk to a caring professional who has the kind of background, education, training, experience, and skill to help us overcome the obstacles keeping us from finding our hope and healing in Christ.

It might be beneficial to you to seek out professional help if any of the following is true for you:

- If your fears could be described as severe, marked, persistent, irrational, uncontrollable, or paralyzing. In other words, if they interfere with your ability to live a normal life.
- If you're experiencing panic attacks (see p. 190).
- If you're going through a major life transition or have recently experienced significant trauma.

- If you find yourself experiencing mood swings, crying uncontrollably, or lashing out at others in anger.
- If you feel you might want to or need to talk to someone—or if people close to you have suggested that you do.
- If you find yourself "self-medicating," using food, alcohol, drugs, sex, or other compulsive behaviors to cope with emotional pain.
- If you have thoughts of death or suicide.
- If your physician has said there is no medical explanation for your symptoms.

How Do I Find a Good Counselor?

Scripture teaches us that it's wise to seek godly counsel, that God has gifted members of the Body of Christ to exhort, encourage, counsel, and advise one another. Some use their gifts on an informal basis; others get specialized training, certification, licensing, or advanced degrees, and choose to make helping others their life's calling—their career and profession.

The first thing to do is pray! Ask God to lead you every step of the way. Then ask people you trust—your friends, your family, your doctor, your pastor—for their recommendations. Get as many as you can. And do your homework. Look up the websites of potential counselors or therapists. Check out their qualifications, their years of experience and areas of expertise. In most cases, you'll want to look for a Christian counselor. But not everyone who claims to be a Christian is one, and not every counselor who is a Christian bases their counseling practice on biblical principles.

Here are a few of the questions you might consider asking a prospective counselor:

- What is your general approach to counseling?
- How do you integrate biblical truths into your counseling?
- Are you involved in a church? Which one and in what role?
- What part does prayer play in the way that you counsel? Do you pray with clients?[1]

You can also find referrals through the American Association of Christian Counselors[2] and the National Christian Counselors Association.[3] Focus on the Family has a free counseling hotline. They can also connect you with a reputable Christian counselor in your area.[4]

Some churches have professional counselors on staff or counseling ministries involving "lay counselors"—members of the congregation who are mature believers and have been through a comprehensive biblical counseling program. Most pastors do offer counseling as well, and pastoral counseling is usually free. One thing to keep in mind: There are many wonderful, godly pastors who have a lot of wisdom, a lot of experience in ministry. They have a heart for people who are hurting, a heart for counseling, as well as a real gift for it—to which many of them add special training to enable them to be even more effective at helping others. But some pastors, well . . . don't.

So again, whenever possible, it's best to get a personal recommendation from someone you trust. And if the first counselor you see isn't as helpful as you hoped, don't give up. Try again. Your healing—your freedom—is worth fighting for!

For more information, see

1. Pastor David Martin, "Choosing a Christian Counselor," http://www.cbn.com/spirituallife/prayerandcounseling/choosing_a_christian_counselor.aspx.
2. American Association of Christian Counselors, www.aacc.net/resources/find-a-counselor/.
3. National Christian Counselors Association, http://www.ncca.org/Directory/search.aspx.
4. Focus on the Family, 1-855-771-HELP (4357), http://www.focusonthefamily.com/counseling/find-a-counselor.aspx.

What about Antianxiety Medication?

Many Christians have serious reservations about taking medication to treat anxiety. If the problem is in essence spiritual, then shouldn't it be addressed from a spiritual perspective and on a spiritual basis? Others believe that since there may be physical causes or at least physical symptoms that coincide with the spiritual issues, medication can be an effective—even lifesaving—tool.

Since the Scripture doesn't say "thou shalt" or "thou shalt not," I think each one of us must prayerfully consider how we believe God is leading us.

Here's What Health-Care Professionals Tell Us:

1. Antianxiety medications (including sleeping pills and muscle relaxants) can provide temporary relief to people suffering from acute anxiety. Notice the words "can" and "temporary." These drugs are not a miracle cure; they do not work for everyone. For some people, they actually have the opposite effect. And even when the drugs work, they do nothing to treat the underlying cause. As soon as a person stops taking the pills, their anxiety returns.

2. It's not safe to stay on antianxiety medication for any substantial length of time, because of all the potential side effects and long-term health risks. In addition, most of the drugs are habit forming (addictive). They can be deadly when taken in combination with alcohol and certain other prescription medications.

3. Antianxiety medications are most effective when taken for a short period of time under close medical supervision and in conjunction with counseling or therapy. At their best, they work like training wheels on a bicycle. They give you a little stability so you can climb back up in the saddle and start pedaling again. Just know that, sooner or later, you've got to be ready to ride on your own.

So is antianxiety medication right for you? Are you prepared to risk the potential side effects? Do you have a plan in place to get the spiritual help and support you need as well? Have you prayed about your decision? Talked to your family? Your doctor?

If you do decide to move forward, make sure your doctor also has a clear plan in mind—which medication he or she will prescribe and for how long. Keep a journal in which you carefully track your medication, dosage, side effects, and symptoms.

And keep looking to Jesus. Ultimately all of our help, our hope, our healing comes from Him.

How Do I Know If I'm Having a Panic Attack—And What Can I Do about It?

Every year, millions of women experience panic attacks brought on by fear, anxiety, stress, grief, or loss. We seem to be particularly vulnerable during major life transitions—graduating from college and entering the workplace, getting married, having a baby, moving, losing a job, going through a divorce, dealing with a significant illness, becoming an empty nester or a full-time caregiver, losing a loved one.

A panic attack can happen anytime, anywhere. It can be a one-time event or a recurring experience. It may or may not have an obvious trigger. In other words, it can happen when you're doing something really stressful—something that scares you—or when you're thinking about things that worry or frighten you. But it can also seem to come out of the blue.

Here Are the Most Common Symptoms:

- hyperventilation, shortness of breath, choking
- heart pounding, heart racing, heart palpitations

- sharp chest pain
- trembling, shaking
- numbness or tingling
- nausea or upset stomach
- dizziness, lightheadedness, feeling faint
- hot flashes, perspiration, or chills
- feeling distant or detached from surroundings
- fear of dying, fear of losing control, fear of going crazy

Many of these symptoms are similar to those of a heart attack, which is one reason panic attacks themselves can be very frightening.

So Is It a Panic Attack or a Heart Attack?

Panic Attack	Heart Attack
Always sudden, intense, dramatic	Usually dull, gradual, slowly building
Chest pain is sharp, localized over the heart, comes and goes with breathing, gone after 10–15 minutes	Chest pain is dull, like a heavy weight sitting on the chest, and may radiate to left arm, neck, jaw, lower back—but does not go away
Nausea, but rarely actual vomiting	Vomiting is common, often repeatedly
Hyperventilating (the key physical symptom of a panic attack that causes all of the others)	May include shortness of breath (tightness in chest, trouble breathing deeply), but hyperventilating only occurs if the heart attack triggers a panic attack!
Tingling all over	Tingling in left arm
Usually peaks at 10 minutes; rarely lasts more than 30 minutes	Lasts longer than 10 minutes; symptoms do not go away
	WOMEN: often experience a sudden, dramatic onset of unusual fatigue or exhaustion

The American Heart Association cautions that many women who have heart disease go undiagnosed, and even some who have heart attacks are misdiagnosed as having panic attacks and sent home from the emergency room without the medical care they need. Apparently our symptoms are often milder and harder to recognize, and the standard tests don't seem to be as reliable for women as they are for men.

So be your own advocate. Find a doctor you can trust and make sure you don't have underlying health issues that are causing your symptoms. Keep in mind that some medications have side effects that can mimic or even trigger panic attacks, including over-the-counter cold medications, weight loss pills, and natural health supplements. Many include caffeine, which in large doses can itself cause anxiety, agitation, restlessness, nausea, heart palpitations, shortness of breath, and chest pains.

When You Are Having a Panic Attack . . .

Remember these three things:

1. Be mindful: As soon as you realize what's happening, remind yourself: "I am not dying. I am not losing my mind. I am not going crazy. This feeling will not last. It will be gone in a few minutes. I can get through it. I can outlast it. I can do this." Better yet, in your heart repeat a simple word or phrase from Scripture, like "peace." Or "be still" (as Jesus told the wind and waves!). Or say the name of Jesus.

2. Breathe deeply: Take control of your breathing. Breathe in and out, slowly to a count of 5. Breathe in through your nose, then blow out through your mouth. Over and over. Slow your breathing, slow your heart rate. As your breathing slows down, try for a longer count of eight or ten seconds.

3. Be still: All the adrenaline coursing through your body, that fight-or-flight response to fear, can make your muscles tense and cause your body to shake. Try to relax your body and be still. Consciously relax your neck and shoulders, unclench your jaw, your fists. Flex your hands and feet. Keep taking deep breaths. If you feel dizzy, put your head between your knees or rest it gently on a table. Close your eyes and breathe. Wait for the feeling to pass. Know that it will—and sooner than you think.

That's it, really. There aren't any special medications or treatments for panic attacks. They're a physical symptom of what is in essence a mental or emotional or spiritual issue. Something is going on inside that you can't handle and your body is telling you—screaming at you—that you need to get help!

If you know what triggered your panic attack, make a note of it. Journal about it. Pray about it. Talk to your family or to a trusted friend. Seek out a qualified Christian counselor (see p. 186).

If your symptoms are severe, if they are interfering with your ability to function, ask your doctor whether it would be appropriate for you to consider taking antianxiety medication for a short period of time—while you make arrangements to begin counseling, for instance (see p. 188).

And eat healthy. Exercise. Rest. Many women have found that taking better care of their physical health has an enormous impact on their mental health—their emotional and spiritual well-being. Honor God by taking care of His temple!

As believers, we recognize that facing fear is also (and in some cases entirely) a spiritual battle. We are under attack, and we've got to fight back with *all* of the resources God has given us. In addition to the strategies mentioned above, use the strategies and weapons we discuss at length in Chapter Six. Learn to take every thought captive (2 Cor. 10:5), to guard your heart and mind (Phil. 4:6–8), to create for yourself an atmosphere of peace, of praise and worship, and of thanksgiving. Prepare for the battle, and you've won before it's begun.

Be encouraged: many of your sisters in Christ have found freedom from fear—and freedom from panic attacks, specifically. Others have learned how to take them in stride and use them as opportunities to lean in close to Jesus and hang on to Him for dear life!

The Apostle Paul described his experience with an ongoing challenge he called a "thorn in the flesh":

> Three different times I begged the Lord to take it away. Each time he said, "My grace is all you need. My power works best in weakness." So now I am glad to boast about my weaknesses, so that the power of Christ can work through me. That's why I take pleasure in my weaknesses, and in the insults, hardships, persecutions, and troubles that I suffer for Christ. For when I am weak, then I am strong. (2 Cor. 12:8–10 NLT)

If You Witness a Friend or Family Member Experiencing a Panic Attack . . .

Use the information you've learned here to help her. And keep in mind a few other important dos and don'ts:

DO make eye contact, squeeze her hand or shoulder, and reassure her with comforting words or phrases, such as, "It's okay, you're going to be okay. Let's take a deep breath together."

DON'T sound like you're rebuking or reprimanding: "You have nothing to be afraid of. Stop panicking. There's nothing wrong. It's all in your head."

DO pray and quote Scripture in your heart as you minister to her, but only say the words out loud if you know that they will be a blessing to her.

DON'T preach at her, don't criticize her for being fearful or condemn her for her lack of faith. Don't claim to know what her problem is and what she needs to do about it!

DO stay with her. When she's ready, offer her a sip of water, some tissues, a cold compress. Accompany her to the restroom and stay close by in case she gets lightheaded. Make sure she gets safely back to a seat or sofa.

DON'T tell her you're going to leave her alone, so she can compose herself. No one wants to be left alone when they're afraid!

DO ask whether she's experienced anything like this before or whether she has any health issues that might be a contributing factor. If this is the first time, ask her to consider going to the hospital or urgent care, just in case. At the very least, strongly encourage her to follow up with her own doctor as soon as possible.

A quick online search will turn up hundreds of web pages that share this same information and advice. Two comprehensive, reputable sites: the American Heart Association (www.heart.org) and WebMD.com.

What Are Some Key Scriptures I Can Memorize?

There are countless Scriptures that challenge us to face our fears with faith, to trust in God and the love He has for us. Meditating on these Scriptures (really reflecting on their meaning and applying them to our lives)—as well as memorizing them—can help us not only face our fears but overcome them. Ideally you want to choose the verses that seem to speak most powerfully and personally to you.

Here Are a Few Verses to Get You Started:

"Peace I leave with you; my peace I give you. I do not give to you as the world gives. Do not let your hearts be troubled and do not be afraid" (John 14:27).

"Cast all your anxiety on him because he cares for you" (1 Pet. 5:7).

"Do not be anxious about anything, but in everything, by prayer and petition, with thanksgiving, present your requests to God. And the peace of God, which transcends all understanding, will guard your hearts and your minds in Christ Jesus" (Phil. 4:6–7).

"For God has not given us a spirit of fear, but of power and of love and of a sound mind" (2 Tim. 1:7 NKJV).

"You will keep in perfect peace all who trust in you, all whose thoughts are fixed on you!" (Isa. 26:3 NLT).

"When I am afraid, I will trust in you" (Ps. 56:3).

"The angel of the LORD encamps around those who fear him, and he delivers them" (Ps. 34:7).

"Be strong and courageous. Do not be afraid or terrified because of them, for the LORD your God goes with you; he will never leave you nor forsake you" (Deut. 31:6).

"The LORD is my light and my salvation— whom shall I fear? The LORD is the stronghold of my life— of whom shall I be afraid?" (Ps. 27:1).

"The God of peace will soon crush Satan under your feet" (Rom. 16:20).

How Can I Help Fearful Children or Grandchildren?

It's one thing to battle fear yourself; it's another to watch children grapple with it. Our hearts go out to them. We know how hard it is. And we feel so helpless. So many parents and grandparents have looked for ways to help their children. A quick Internet search will pull up hundreds of articles and websites full of ideas and practical suggestions.

Here Are a Few Basics:

Pray. And then pray. And then pray some more. Seriously! Ask God for wisdom every single day, with every single incident or issue that comes up. Every child is different; every situation is different. It takes so much wisdom to know what to do and what not to do, what to say and what not to say. To find the balance between comforting children and challenging them to learn and grow. Thankfully God promises to give us all the wisdom we need, if we ask for it (James 1:5)!

Learn to face your own fears and lead by example. Teach your children the same principles, the same Scriptures, the same strategies that are helping you. Just adapt them a little—use examples and illustrations that are age appropriate.

And keep in mind the following dos and don'ts:

DO acknowledge that your children's fear (the feeling) is real, even if the danger is not. Be comforting and reassuring.

DON'T dismiss their fears, ridicule them, or talk openly about their fears in front of others.

DO ask questions to see whether you can figure out where the fear is coming from and what it's really about. Did they hear something at school? Did they see something on TV? Often there's more to the story.

DON'T shut them down with statements like, "I don't want to hear any more of this nonsense! Stop being silly!"

DO listen carefully. Take your children's fears seriously. Sometimes kids have good reason to be afraid. They might be trying to tell you something.

DON'T overreact. Don't get hysterical or panicky or blow things out of proportion. Someone needs to be the grown-up, and at least *appear* calm and in control!

DO take reasonable, practical steps to help your children feel safe. For example, you might give them a nightlight or a flashlight at bedtime. Let them take a stuffed animal buddy to a doctor's appointment or a family picture and a list of emergency contacts when they're away from home. Simple things that give them some peace of mind.

DON'T assume they'll just outgrow their fears (even though many do). Don't hesitate to seek professional help if their fears seem extreme, prolonged, or paralyzing—or if they coincide with a major life transition or trauma, such as a parent's divorce or remarriage, death of a loved one, chronic illness, or becoming the victim of crime, tragedy, or abuse.

Other Helpful Tips:

Take advantage of teachable moments. Explain the things you can. Together, why not learn about dogs or frogs or spiders or whatever frightens your children? Sometime other than bath time, use different sized toys to show them what things can and cannot go down the drain. The children's section of your local library will have lots of books and videos created especially to help children face their fears. Check them out!

Look for opportunities to build your children's confidence, give them a sense of accomplishment, and inspire a spirit of adventure. Get them involved in games, sports, activities, crafts, and other things they're interested in, things that they do well.

Try to strike a balance. You don't want to force children into scary situations, bully them into taking on a challenge they are not ready to face, not prepared to handle. Then again you don't want to keep them from learning how to face their fears and overcome them—an important life skill! If you're too eager to let them off the hook, you can unintentionally communicate that 1) there really is something to fear (when there isn't) and 2) you don't think they can handle it (you see them as fragile, incapable, inferior—which is how they will come to view themselves).

For children who have meltdowns—child-sized panic attacks—teach them to stop and think about what's happening to them. Have them rate their fear on a scale of 1–10 (or for younger children, how "full" of fear they feel—"up to my knees" . . . "up to my tummy"). Practice breathing with them, slowly, in and out to a count of five. Remind them that feelings are important signals—they tell us something is going on inside. But they don't always tell us the truth. We need to think carefully before we decide to believe them.

Pitfalls Christian Parents Should Avoid

Making it sound like praying makes all our problems go away. Telling children if they're scared, they should just pray, and that will make the feeling disappear. Really? Is that what works for you? (Why are you reading this book?) Praying absolutely does help! But it's not the only thing we can or should do.

Being too real with our kids. It's okay to admit that sometimes we're frightened, too. We may need to be truthful about difficult situations we face. But we don't need to confide all of our deepest, darkest fears in full detail to our "amazingly mature kids." There are some burdens they really shouldn't have to carry—no matter how mature they are.

Promising we won't ever let anything bad happen or that God won't ever let anything bad happen to them. That's not a promise you can keep. Your children need to be able to trust you and trust God. So tell them the truth: Most of the things we fear will never happen to us. Mommy and Daddy are watching over us. And, more importantly, God is watching over us. He protects us from all kinds of things, all the time, even when we don't realize it. But sometimes bad things do happen. Sometimes, for reasons we don't fully understand, God allows bad things to happen. But He promises that He will always be with us; He will never leave us or forsake us. He will help us. And He has a way of bringing good out of the worst things that happen to us. One day we will be with Him in our forever home in heaven, where there is no fear, no pain, no suffering. Only love and peace and joy and laughter! That's what we long for and look forward to.

Music for Young Children

I used to be a preschool and elementary school teacher, and, when I was teaching in Christian schools, I loved to keep praise and worship music playing softly in the background throughout the day. It made my classroom feel like a warm, happy, safe place to be. It had such a calming influence on my students! I'd often hear the children singing the words of the songs in the hallway or on the playground—even though we'd never made a conscious effort to learn them. I often caught myself singing them, too!

Playtime, naptime, drive-time, nighttime—these are all good times to strengthen our hearts and nourish our spirits with the truth of God's Word.

Here are just a few of my personal favorites for young children. (All of these albums are available on iTunes and online sources.)

- *Kids of the Kingdom* and *Follow the Leader*, by Annie Herring
- *The Donut Man*—Songs That Teach, Songs That Praise series, by Rob Evans
- The Praise Baby Collection, by Contemporary praise & worship sung by kids for kids
- *Hide 'Em in Your Heart: Bible Memory Melodies, Vols. 1 and 2,* by Steve Green
- *Sleep Sound in Jesus: Gentle Lullabies For Baby*, by Michael Card
- *Bedtime Prayers: Lullabies and Peaceful Worship,* by Twila Paris

If you have older children, encourage them to create their own playlists—songs that bring them peace, songs that fill them with joy, songs that remind them to be strong in the Lord!

What If My Child Is Shy?

I can relate! As I've already shared, this was one of my paralyzing fears growing up. Entire books have been written on how to help children overcome feeling shy, fearing rejection, and being anxious about fitting in. Let me just share a few thoughts here.

It's important to remember that being a quieter, more thoughtful (introspective and reflective) person—as opposed to being a bubbly, life-of-the-party, never-met-a-stranger people person—is not in and of itself a "problem"! It's a God-given temperament, with its own unique strengths and weaknesses. And sometimes being "shy"—slow to warm up to and embrace total strangers—is just good common sense!

Being shy is a problem when it keeps us from being able to function in the world we live in—when we are unable to interact with the people we meet on a daily basis in a normal, healthy way.

Often at the root of behavior we consider "shy" is the fear of being embarrassed or humiliated. Not knowing what to say. Realizing that if we express ourselves awkwardly, we risk being mocked or ridiculed, criticized, or misunderstood. We could be rejected. Maybe we already have been.

Many shy kids simply need help figuring out how to approach others, how to start a conversation and keep it going, what kinds of things to talk about. This is something you can teach them, something you can model, something that together you can practice. Do a little role playing in the car on the way to school or to a birthday party or sleepover. Encourage your children to practice their social skills on playdates, at karate or ballet, in Sunday school or alongside other family members in group activities or volunteer projects.

When I was a teenager, my parents constantly reminded me that the popular kids were not nearly as secure or confident as they appeared. That deep down everyone has issues. And most people are too focused on their own issues to care about or even notice yours. They said that if I looked, I would find other kids who were alone, other kids who needed a friend. What if I decided to be that friend? What if I reached out to others, instead of waiting for them to reach out to me? My dad taught me that most people like to talk about themselves and that if you ask questions and really listen, if you show that you care, you make friends. One day I tried it, and I was amazed—it worked! Later I even got up the courage to approach some of the popular kids and try it with them. Guess what? It worked with them, too! Talk about a revelation.

When we focus on being kind and loving and compassionate toward others, we forget ourselves—in a good way. We forget to be self-conscious. We're not so self-focused, so self-absorbed. And we become our best, truest selves (Eph. 4:23–24). For all of us, it's a process, a lifelong journey.

Recommended Resources

Facing fear is such a challenge for so many of us! The good news is that we're not alone. And there are hundreds of books and Bible studies, CDs and DVDs, workshops, websites, and even smartphone apps that can give us insight into just about every aspect of facing fear, from every imaginable perspective. In addition to those I've mentioned in the text and in the endnotes, I've included just a few other resources I personally recommend here. You can also check out www.WhatWomenShouldKnow.org for additional resources as I run across them—or as they're recommended to me by readers like you!

For Further Reading

Hind's Feet on High Places, by Hannah Hurnard (Tyndale, 1975).

One of the best-known, most beloved Christian classics on facing fear and finding victory, this beautiful allegory has comforted and strengthened millions of believers for generations. Don't miss the author's personal testimony at the end, or the lesser-known sequel, *Mountains of Spices*!

Streams in the Desert, by L. B. Cowman, updated by Jim Reimann (Zondervan, 1997).

Another beloved Christian classic, this daily devotional is full of inspiration, comfort, courage, and strength for those walking through dark times.

Becoming a Brave New Woman: Step into God's Adventure for You, by Pam Farrel (Harvest House, 2009).

We've been learning to face our fears. Pam Farrel challenges us to take the next steps—to trust God and embrace His adventure, move through life with boldness and daring, and achieve the dreams He's given us. "Show me the size of your God and I will show you the size of your confidence," Farrel often says. "Big God, big confidence. Big God, big courage. Big God, big-on bravery!"

Live a Praying Life!, by Jennifer Kennedy Dean (New Hope, 2011).

Sometimes we've been afraid to trust God because we're not sure He hears our prayers, we're not sure if or how or why He answers them. We're not even sure we know the "right" way to pray. Jennifer answers all of these questions and more in a thoroughly biblical, thoroughly practical, truly enlightening—even life-changing way.

Miracle on Hope Hill: And Other True Stories of God's Love, by Carol Kent and Jennie Afman Dimkoff (Howard Books, 2011).

Nourish your faith with this inspiring collection of true stories of God's love and comfort, wisdom and guidance, healing, and intervention in the lives of ordinary people like you and me.

Don't Waste the Pain: Learning to Grow through Suffering, by David Lyons and Linda Lyons Richardson (NavPress, 2010).

Brother and sister David and Linda share in a very real, honest way what God has taught them through their battles with the disease that so many of us fear—cancer. In David's case, the aggressive cancer that took the life of his young son, and in Linda's an ongoing thirteen-year battle with ovarian cancer. As the book cover describe it, "Searing pain, abundant peace!"

The God of All Comfort: Finding Your Way into His Arms, by Dee Brestin (Zondervan, 2009).

For those of us who are grieving the loss of a loved one and fear that the grief will never end—that we will not survive it. Dee Brestin shares her own story, as well as countless psalms and hymns that point us to the God who is our comfort and strength.

No More Christian Nice Girl: When Just Being Nice—Instead of Good—Hurts You, Your Family, and Your Friends, by Paul Coughlin and Jennifer D. Degler, (Bethany House, 2010).

Our fear—fear of rejection, fear of criticism, fear of risk, fear of loss—can keep us tied up in knots, trying so hard to be "nice" that we can't say no to things we don't want to do and yes to the things we do! Learn how being good (being godly, being Christlike) is so much better than being nice.

The Emotionally Destructive Relationship: Seeing It, Stopping It, Surviving It, by Leslie Vernick (Harvest House, 2007).
The Emotionally Destructive Marriage: How to Find Your Voice and Reclaim Your Hope, by Leslie Vernick (Multnomah / Waterbrook, 2013).

Women who are in abusive relationships have reason to be afraid. That fear is a warning that we need to get help—and (often) get ourselves and our children out of harm's way. Christian counselor Leslie Vernick offers practical, biblically grounded advice for those of us in difficult relationships, helping us recognize abusive behaviors (meant to control, punish, and hurt), set appropriate boundaries, determine when to keep trying and when to shift our approach, how to get safe and stay safe, and find hope and healing as we rebuild our identity in Christ.

The Hiding Place, 35th Anniversary Edition, by Corrie Ten Boom with John and Elizabeth Sherrill (Chosen Books, 2006).
A Chance to Die: The Life and Legacy of Amy Carmichael, by Elisabeth Elliot (Revell, 1987).

Corrie Ten Boom was a Dutch woman who hid Jews from the Nazis. She survived the horrors of the concentration camps to travel the world preaching the Gospel and the power of forgiveness. Amy Carmichael poured out her life on the mission field in India, rescuing orphaned and abandoned children from slavery and prostitution. The stories of these two courageous women can't help but inspire you!

Persuasion, by Jane Austen (1817)
The Scarlet Pimpernel, by Baroness Orczy (1905)
The Blue Castle, by L. M. Montgomery (1926)

Just for fun—three of my all-time favorite classic novels featuring women who suddenly decide NOT to live their lives in fear (of others' opinions, of an uncertain future, or of certain death) and discover a courage and strength they didn't know they had!

For Listening:

The Bible
There are many different audio versions of Scripture available, in a variety of translations and formats (mp3, CD, DVD). You can choose the entire Bible, the Old Testament, the New Testament, just one particular book of the Bible, or even a selection of devotional Scripture readings. Try to listen to a few online or at your local Christian bookstore, to see whether you prefer a dramatized version (with passages acted out by different actors and dramatic background music) or simple narration.

Prayers & Meditations
One Christmas, as a gift to my friends and family, I recorded some of our favorite Scriptures and Scripture-based prayers. Christian composer and recording artist Andre Lefebvre graciously gave me permission to use his beautiful instrumental music as the setting. The friends and family who received the CD shared it with their friends and family—and I started getting requests for more CDs from people all over the country! Many say they listen to the album when they (or their children)

have trouble sleeping. You can listen to and download all of the prayers for free from my radio ministry website: http://www.takeittoheartradio.com/free/

Music for Your Playlists

You may already have a number of much-loved songs or albums that you listen to when you need to be reminded of God's presence, His protection, and His peace. But if you're looking for some new songs to add to your playlist, keeping our "facing fear" theme in mind, here are a few of my personal favorites:

Albums:

Draw Me Close: Songs of Worship and *Comfort*, by Kathy Troccoli
Hymns & Meditations, by Fernando Ortega

Songs:

"The Deer's Cry," by Lisa Kelly
"Be Still My Soul," by David Archuleta
"You Are My Hiding Place," by Selah
"Give Me Jesus," by Fernando Ortega
"Cares Chorus," by Kelly Willard
"Hiding Place," by Steven Curtis Chapman
"Made Me Glad," by Sheila Walsh
"For This I Have Jesus," by Graham Kendrick
"Psalm Twenty-Three," by Kathy Troccoli
"Man of the Tombs," by Bob Bennett
"In Christ Alone," by Keith and Kristyn Getty
"A Mighty Fortress Is Our God," by Steve Green
"It Is Well," by Wintley Phipps

"I Am," by Jill Phillips
"Hold Me, Jesus," by Rich Mullins
"Jesus King of Angels," by Sheila Walsh
"Barocha," by Michael Card

Praise and worship, hymns, classical music, instrumental music, even your favorite movie soundtracks can also be uplifting and inspiring! Find what blesses your heart or ministers to your spirit most, and listen to it as often as you can.

Notes

Chapter 3

1. Matthew Henry, *Zondervan NIV Matthew Henry Commentary* (Grand Rapids, MI: Zondervan, 1992), 334.

Chapter 4

1. Earl Nightingale, "The Fog of Worry (Only 8% of Worries Are Worth It," *The Essence of Success*. Accessed January 15, 2013. http://www.nightingale.com/articles/the-fog-of-worry-only-8-of-worries-are-worth-it/

2. Mrs. Charles E. Cowman, *Streams in the Desert* (Grand Rapids, MI: Zondervan, 1925), December 1 entry.

Chapter 5

1. John Piper, *Spectacular Sins: And Their Global Purpose in the Glory of Christ* (Wheaton, IL: Crossway Books, 2008).

2. Corrie Ten Boom, *The Hiding Place: 35th Anniversary Edition* (Ada, MI: Chosen Books, 2006) 43–44.

Chapter 6

1. Sue Manning, "Dogs Help Scaredy-Cat Cheetahs Survive," *The Sarasota Herald Tribune*, Associated Press, February 12, 2013.

2. Pam Farrel, *Becoming a Brave New Woman* (Eugene, OR: Harvest House, 2009), 111.

Chapter 7

1. Randy Alcorn, *Heaven* (Carol Stream, IL: Tyndale, 2004), 28.

Chapter 8

1. Jennifer Kennedy Dean, *The Praying Life: Open Your Life to God's Power and Provision* (Birmingham, AL: New Hope, 2011), 151.

Calling women to a deeper life. A richer, fuller life.
The kind of life that comes from a deeper, richer,
fuller relationship with the Author of life—Jesus Christ.

This is not only the heart of Christin's message, but her life's passion.

Christin Ditchfield is an accomplished educator, author, conference speaker, and host of the syndicated radio program, Take It To Heart!®, heard daily on hundreds of stations across the United States and around the world.

She has written dozens of best-selling gospel tracts and hundreds of columns, essays, and articles for national and international magazines. Christin is the author of more than sixty-five books, translated into half a dozen languages, including *A Family Guide to Narnia, A Family Guide to the Bible, The Three Wise Women: A Christmas Reflection,* and *A Way With Words: What Women Should Know about the Power They Possess.*

For over twenty-five years, Christin has been speaking at conferences, retreats, banquets, and brunches. She is a frequent guest on radio and television programs such as *Midday Connection, Truth Talk Live, HomeWord* with Jim Burns, Dr.

D. James Kennedy's *Truths That Transform* and *FamilyLife Today*. Christin holds a master's degree in Biblical Theology. If you enjoyed this book, be sure to check out Christin's blog:

http://WhatWomenShouldKnow.org

And listen to her radio broadcasts:

www.TakeItToHeartRadio.com

Or follow her on:

http://facebook.com/christinditchfield

http://twitter.com/authorchristin

http://pinterest.com/authorchristin